First World War
and Army of Occupation
War Diary
France, Belgium and Germany

50 DIVISION
Divisional Troops
Machine Gun Corps
50 Battalion
1 April 1918 - 30 April 1919

WO95/2823/3

The Naval & Military Press Ltd
www.nmarchive.com
Published in association with The National Archives

Published by

The Naval & Military Press Ltd

Unit 10 Ridgewood Industrial Park,

Uckfield, East Sussex,

TN22 5QE England

Tel: +44 (0) 1825 749494

www.naval-military-press.com

www.nmarchive.com

This diary has been reprinted in facsimile from the original. Any imperfections are inevitably reproduced and the quality may fall short of modern type and cartographic standards.

© Crown Copyright
Images reproduced by permission of The National Archives, London, England, 2015.

Contents

Document type	Place/Title	Date From	Date To
Heading	WO95/2823 50 Div 50 Bn M.G.C. Apr 18-Apr 19		
Heading	50 Bn Machine Gun Corps. 1918 Apr-1919 Apl		
Heading	50th Battalion Machine Gun Comps April 1918		
War Diary	Saleux	01/04/1918	02/04/1918
War Diary	Dominois	03/04/1918	05/04/1918
War Diary	Robecq Sheet 36 A	06/04/1918	17/04/1918
War Diary	Petit Quiestede	18/04/1918	26/04/1918
War Diary	Ref Map Soissons Sheet 22	27/04/1918	30/04/1918
Heading	B. Company		
War Diary	Argoules Sur-Somme	01/04/1918	03/04/1918
War Diary	Argoules And Robecq	04/04/1918	04/04/1918
War Diary	Robecq and Mt Bernandon	05/04/1918	07/04/1918
War Diary	Robermetz	08/04/1918	08/04/1918
War Diary	Robermetz And Doulieu (F.30.c.3.5)	09/04/1918	09/04/1918
War Diary	Gde Marquette Farm E.7a.0.8 (36a 1/40,000)	10/04/1918	11/04/1918
War Diary	Morbecque	12/04/1918	12/04/1918
War Diary	Chiennes	13/04/1918	15/04/1918
War Diary	Chiennes and Quiestede A.28.c.6.4	16/04/1918	16/04/1918
War Diary	Quiestede	17/04/1918	19/04/1918
War Diary	Quiestede and Ecques	20/04/1918	20/04/1918
War Diary	Ecques G.1.d.5.9 (36a 1/40,000)	21/04/1918	26/04/1918
War Diary	Grugny	27/04/1918	30/04/1918
Heading	C. Company		
War Diary		01/04/1918	04/04/1918
War Diary	Robecq	04/04/1918	13/04/1918
War Diary	In The Field	14/04/1918	25/04/1918
War Diary		01/04/1918	12/04/1918
Heading	D. Company		
War Diary	Robecq Ref Sheet 36a 1/40,000	07/04/1918	08/04/1918
War Diary	Estaires	09/04/1918	09/04/1918
War Diary	Aviation Ground L.32.a.7.7	10/04/1918	10/04/1918
War Diary	Robermetz	11/04/1918	12/04/1918
War Diary	La Motte Chateau	13/04/1918	15/04/1918
War Diary	Gd Quiestede	16/04/1918	25/04/1918
War Diary	Lapugnoy	27/04/1918	27/04/1918
War Diary	Crugny	28/04/1918	28/04/1918
Heading	War Diary Of 50th Batt. M.G.C. From May 1st 1918 To May 31st 1918 Volume II		
War Diary	Crugny	01/05/1918	04/05/1918
War Diary	Merval	05/05/1918	07/05/1918
War Diary	In The Line	08/05/1918	31/05/1918
Miscellaneous	Corrigenda No. 1 To Organization Of 50th Bn. M.G.C. In The Beaurieux Sector.	22/05/1918	22/05/1918
Miscellaneous	50th Battn. Machine Gun Corps. Operation Order No. 1 Appendix I	04/05/1918	04/05/1918
Miscellaneous	Operation Order No. 503 Appendix 2	05/05/1918	05/05/1918
Miscellaneous	March Table.		
Miscellaneous	Organization Of The 50th M.G. Bn. In The Beaurieux Sector Appendix IV	21/05/1918	21/05/1918

Miscellaneous	50th Battalion Machine Gun Corps. Order No. 3 Appendix 3	14/05/1918	14/05/1918
Miscellaneous			
Heading	War Diary Of 50th Batt. M.G.C. From June 1st 1918 To June 30th 1918 Volume III		
War Diary	In The Field	01/06/1918	30/06/1918
Heading	War Diary Of 50th Batt. M.G.C. From July V1st 1918 To July 31st 1918 Volume IV		
War Diary		01/07/1918	31/07/1918
Miscellaneous	50th Bn. M.G.C. Order No. 8 Appendix No. 1 (B)		
Miscellaneous	50th Bn. M.G.C. Order No. 9 Appendix No. 1(C)	02/07/1918	02/07/1918
Miscellaneous	50th Bn. M.G.C. Order No. 10 Appendix No. 2	06/07/1918	06/07/1918
Miscellaneous	Appendix No. 3 "A" Coy. "B" Coy.	09/07/1918	09/07/1918
Miscellaneous	50th Bn. M.G.C. Order No. 11 Appendix No. 4	28/07/1918	28/07/1918
Heading	War Diary Of 50th Bn M.G.C. From August 1st 1918 To August 31st 1918 Volume 4		
War Diary	At Rust	01/08/1918	02/08/1918
War Diary	In The Field	03/08/1918	31/08/1918
Miscellaneous			
Miscellaneous	50th Bn. M.G.C. Order No. 12 Appendix No. 1	31/07/1918	31/07/1918
Miscellaneous	50th Bn. M.G.C. Order No. 13 Appendix No. 2	01/08/1918	01/08/1918
Miscellaneous	50th Bn. M.G.C. Order No. 14 Appendix No. 3	08/08/1918	08/08/1918
Miscellaneous	50th Bn. M.G.C. Order No. 15 Appendix No. 4		
Miscellaneous	50th Bn. M.G.C. Order No. 16 Appendix No. 5	10/08/1918	10/08/1918
Miscellaneous	50th Bn. M.G.C. Order No. 17 Appendix No. 6	13/08/1918	13/08/1918
Miscellaneous	50th Bn. M.G.C. Order No. 18 Appendix No. 7	14/08/1918	14/08/1918
Miscellaneous	50th Bn. M.G.C. Order No. 19 Appendix No. 8	18/08/1918	18/08/1918
Miscellaneous	50th Bn. M.G.C. Order No. 20 Appendix No. 9	19/08/1918	19/08/1918
Heading	War Diary Of 50th Bn. M.G.C. From Sept 1st 1918 To Sept 30th 1918 Volume VI		
War Diary		01/09/1918	30/09/1918
Miscellaneous	50th Bn. M.G.C. Order No. 22 Appendix No. 1	07/09/1918	07/09/1918
Miscellaneous	50th Bn. M.G.C. Order No. 23 Appendix No. 2	15/09/1918	15/09/1918
Miscellaneous	Schedule With Order No. 23	15/09/1918	15/09/1918
Miscellaneous	50th Bn. M.G.C. Order No. 24 Appendix 3	27/09/1918	27/09/1918
Miscellaneous	50th Bn. M.G.C. Order No. 25 Appendix 4	28/09/1918	28/09/1918
Miscellaneous	War Diary Of 50th Bn. M.G.C. From Oct 1st 1918 To Oct 31st 1918 Volume VII		
War Diary	At Rust	01/10/1918	01/10/1918
War Diary	In The Line	02/10/1918	08/10/1918
War Diary	At Rust	09/10/1918	10/10/1918
War Diary	In The Line	11/10/1918	31/10/1918
Miscellaneous	50th Bn. M.G.C. Order No. 5 Appendix V	24/05/1918	24/05/1918
Miscellaneous	50th Battalion M.G.C. Appendix VI	02/06/1918	02/06/1918
Miscellaneous	Corrigenda No. 1 To 50th Battn M.G. Corps. Order No. 7	01/06/1918	01/06/1918
Miscellaneous	March Table To Accompany 50th Bn. M.G. Corps Order No. 7		
Miscellaneous	50th Battn. M.G. Corps Order No. 7 Appendix 1 (A)	30/06/1918	30/06/1918
Miscellaneous	50th Bn. M.G.C. Order No. 26 Appendix 2	01/10/1918	01/10/1918
Miscellaneous	50th Bn. Machine Gun Corps. Appendix No. 1	21/10/1918	21/10/1918
Miscellaneous	50th Bn. Machine Gun Corps. Appendix No. 1	20/10/1918	20/10/1918
Miscellaneous	50th Division Operation Order No. 250 Appendix No 3	03/10/1918	03/10/1918
Miscellaneous	50th Bn. M.G.C. Order No. 27 Appendix No. 4	04/10/1918	04/10/1918
Miscellaneous	50th Bn. M.G.C. Order No. 28 Appendix No. 5	07/10/1918	07/10/1918
Miscellaneous	50th Bn. M.G.C. Order No. 29 Appendix No. 6	08/10/1918	08/10/1918

Miscellaneous	Amendment No. 1 To Operation Order No. 29 Appendix No. 6	07/10/1918	07/10/1918
Miscellaneous	50th Bn. M.G.C. Order No. 30 Appendix 7	14/10/1918	14/10/1918
Miscellaneous	Preliminary Instructions For Operations To Take Place On Z Day. Appendix No. 8	15/09/1918	15/09/1918
Miscellaneous	50th Bn. M.G.C. Order No. 31 Appendix No. 9	16/10/1918	16/10/1918
Miscellaneous	Addendum No. 1 To 50th Bn. M.G.C. Order No. 31 Appendix No. 9		
Miscellaneous	50th Bn. M.G.C. Order No. 33 Appendix No. 11	19/10/1918	19/10/1918
Miscellaneous	50th Bn. M.G.C. Order No. 12 Appendix No.16	17/10/1918	17/10/1918
Miscellaneous		16/10/1918	16/10/1918
Miscellaneous	50th Bn. M.G.C. Order No. 34 Appendix No. 12	21/10/1918	21/10/1918
Miscellaneous	50th Bn. M.G.C. Order No. 35 Appendix No. 13	28/10/1918	28/10/1918
Miscellaneous	50th Bn. M.G.C. War Diary Vol 8		
War Diary	In The Line	01/11/1918	30/11/1918
Miscellaneous	50th Bn. Machine Gun Corps. Appendix No. 1 (A)	03/11/1918	03/11/1918
Miscellaneous	50th Bn. Machine Gun Corps Appendix No. I	02/11/1918	02/11/1918
Miscellaneous	50th Bn. M.G.C. Order No. 37 Appendix No. 2	04/11/1918	04/11/1918
Miscellaneous	50th Bn. M.G.C. Order No. 38 Appendix No. 3	06/11/1918	06/11/1918
Miscellaneous	50th Bn. M.G.C. Order No. 39 Appendix No. 4	10/11/1918	10/11/1918
Miscellaneous	50th Bn. Machine Gun Corps Order No. 40 Appendix No. 5	29/11/1918	29/11/1918
Heading	50th Bn. M.G.C. War Diary Vol 9 December 1st To 31st 1918		
War Diary	At Rust	01/12/1918	31/12/1918
Miscellaneous	50th Bn. M.G.C. Order No. 41 Appendix No. 1	04/12/1918	04/12/1918
Miscellaneous	Every Gun Number Must Know		
Miscellaneous	50th Bn. Machine Gun Corps Order No. 42	15/12/1918	15/12/1918
Miscellaneous	March Table		
Miscellaneous	Appendix No. II to All Recipients of C.C. No. 42.	16/12/1918	16/12/1918
Heading	War Diary 50th Batt M.G. Corps Vol IX January 1919		
War Diary	Saultain	01/01/1919	31/01/1919
Heading	War Diary Of 50th Battalion Machine Gun Corps. From 1st February 1919 To 28th February 1919 Volume X		
War Diary	Saultain	01/02/1919	28/02/1919
Heading	War Diary Of 50th Battalion Machine Gun Corps From March 1st 1919 To March 31st 1919 Volume XII		
War Diary	Beaudignies	01/03/1919	31/03/1919
Heading	War Diary Of 50th Battalion Machine Gun Corps From April 1st 1919 To April 30th 1919 Volume XIII		
War Diary	Beaudignies	01/04/1919	30/04/1919

WO95/2823
50 Div
50 Bn M.G.C
Apr '18 – Apr '19

(3)

50 DIVISION

50 BN. MACHINE GUN CRR

1918 APL — 1919 APL

50th Divisional Troops

50th BATTALION

MACHINE GUN CORPS

APRIL 1918.

WAR DIARY
or
INTELLIGENCE SUMMARY.
(Erase heading not required.)

Army Form C. 2118.

A Coy

Place	Date	Hour	Summary of Events and Information	Remarks and references to Appendices
April 1918	1st		Coy. Resting	
SALEUX	2d		Entrained at SALEUX at 4.30 am and proceeded to RUE, detraining at 11.30 am. Proceeded by march route via VRON to DOMINOIS	App I
DOMINOIS	3rd		Company resting. Received 50% Dn. O.O. no 191	
	4th		Teams which had been attached to the 20th Division rejoined.	
	5th		Entrained at DOURIEZ at 10.0 pm and proceeded to LILLERS arr 5.7 P.M. PERNES and AIRE. Detrained near LILLERS and marched to ROBECQ.	
ROBECQ	6th		Coy. Resting	
Sheet 36 A.	7th		Company reorganising. Guns etc cleaned and overhauled.	
	8th		Moved from ROBECQ by march route through MERVILLE to CHAPELLE DUVELLE	
	9th		Coy remained all day at CHAPELLE DUVELLE until 7.0 pm. Nos 1, 2 & 3 Sections moved forward to take up positions on the line. Transport and no 4 Section moved to LES LAURIERS.	App II
	10th		Positions taken up on a line from 24 A 2.4 to 23 B 0.5. Orders received from 149th Infy Bde sdns to send 4 guns to cover the 1/4th Bn Northumberland Fusiliers in ESTAIRES. Enemy attacked ESTAIRES, these positions being held.	

CHornpunzel

WAR DIARY
or
INTELLIGENCE SUMMARY.
(Erase heading not required.)

Army Form C. 2118.

Place	Date	Hour	Summary of Events and Information	Remarks and references to Appendices
Sheet 36A			until the morning of the 11th. Casualties. 2nd Lt A.M. JONES M.C. Wounded. 2nd Lt G. BURGOINE - Wounded, 2nd Lt E. HAZELEY - Missing. 1 O.R. Killed 4 O.R. Wounded.	
	11th		Coy withdrawn to position in 10 c 2.1 to 9 d 2.0, to cover Coys Re-inforcement battalion. These positions were held until 6.0 P.M. when they were withdrawn with the 149th Infy Bde. Position were taken up on a line 7a 3.8 to 11d 7.4. Severe fighting took place during the day the line was withdrawn in the evening. Company withdrawn from the line and proceeded to LAMOTTE-AU-BOIS. Casualties. 1 O.R. Killed 13 O.R. Wounded	
	12th			
	13th		Coy Resting 10 O.R. Missing	
	14th		Coy resting. Guns cleaned etc.	
	15th		do do O.O. 198 received	APP III
	16th		Moved to the WITTES-FIRE area. Coy proceeded by march route to PETIT QUESTEDE.	
	17th		Coy re-organising. Guns, opt. park & belts overhauled	Appendix

T./2134. Wt. W708-776. 500000. 4/15. Sir J. C. & S.

Army Form C. 2118.

WAR DIARY
or
INTELLIGENCE SUMMARY.
(Erase heading not required.)

Instructions regarding War Diaries and Intelligence Summaries are contained in F. S. Regs., Part II. and the Staff Manual respectively. Title pages will be prepared in manuscript.

Place	Date	Hour	Summary of Events and Information	Remarks and references to Appendices
PETIT QUESTEDE	18th		Guns Belts etc overhauled and cleaned.	
	19th		Coy. Inspected by R.S.C. Division.	
	20th		Embus cleaned. Squad Drill etc carried out.	
	21st		do do Coy. Inspected by C.O. 50th Bn. M.G.C.	
	22nd		Saluting Drill, Arms Drill etc carried out.	
	23rd		do	
	24th		do	
	25th		Received O.O. no 201 Belts overhauled and filled. Recd reg ord'ys Bn Order No 19	App # 5
	26th		Moved by march route to MAMETZ. Entrained at 4.0AM and proceeded to PERNES. Entrained at PERNES at 9.45AM and proceeded to FERE-EN-TOIDENOIS Marched to SERINGES (AISNE) arriving at 12 midnight.	
Ref Map SOISSONS Sht 22	27th			
	28th		Departed from SERINGES at 10 p.m. and marched via LAGERY & CRUGNY arriving at 6.30 P.M.	
	29th		Coy resting.	
"	30th		Coy inspected by Battalion C.O. (Major J Morris 25.O) Gun Drill etc carried out	

CHMangrove

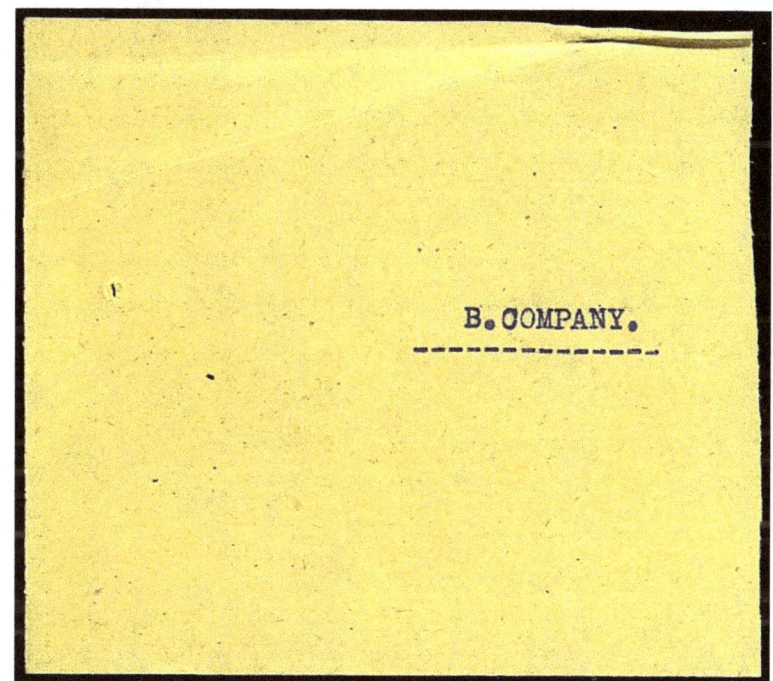

"B" COMPANY WAR DIARY of 50th Bn: MACHINE GUN CORPS. VOLUME 2nd APRIL 1918
INTELLIGENCE SUMMARY.
Army Form C. 2118.
CONFIDENTIAL

Place	Date APRIL.	Hour	Summary of Events and Information	Remarks and references to Appendices
ARGOULES-SUR-SOMME.	1st.	3am. 3pm.	Coy. less Transport entrained at SALEAUX and proceeded to RUE arriving there at 12noon. Thence by march route to ARGOULES a distance of 16 Kms. Arriving there at 3pm. Transport moved out both by light Pole group from BOURDON to DONVAST by road, where a halt was made for the night. Weather good.	006 4
"	2nd.	11.30am.	Transport, less one limbered wagon attached to 20th Div: rejoined Company limbers cleaned during afternoon and deficiencies indented for. Supplies Pte out dead as Coy: is now dependant on its own Transport for food. Moves Limbers repacked 53 Wards joined the unit as reinforcements from Base. Weather good.	006 4
"	3rd.		Day spent in cleaning up transport. Warning Order received at 3pm and Coy: moved one hour notice. Transport moved off at 4/pm and proceeded to WILLIMAN where a halt was made for the night. Coy: retained one blanket per man. Weather good.	006 4
ARGOULES and ROBECQ.	4th.	11am	Coy. less Transport moved off and embraced at DOURIEZ and proceeded to ROBECQ. Transport proceeded to FIEFS. A riding horse was badly kicked and was shot by M.V.S.	006 4
ROBECQ and Mt BERNANDON.	5th.		Transport arrived at Mt BERNANDON. Limbers parked at ROBECQ but animals stabled at Mt BERNANDON. Weather dull, raining during afternoon. Officers arrived from Base as reinforcements (Lieut C.J.BURTON + 2/Lieuts WM.GRANT) Very freezing.	006 4
"	6th.		All guns and Gun kit cleaned. Belt Boxes received from Batt. Belt filling and repacking of limbers during afternoon. Weather bad.	006 4
"	7th.		Warning Order received. S.A.A Magor Gun Batt: and belt boxes to complete Limbers. Washed and oiled, and repacked ready for next. Weather good. OHunsCh	006 4

"B" COMPANY.
VOLUME 24.

50TH BN. M. GUN CORPS.
SHEET 2. APRIL 1918.
REF. SHEETS 36 and 36a/1/40,000.

Army Form C. 2118.

WAR DIARY or INTELLIGENCE SUMMARY.
(Erase heading not required.)

Place	Date APRIL	Hour	Summary of Events and Information	Remarks and references to Appendices
ROBERMETZ.	8th.	4/5am	Coy. with transport moved off and proceeded to ROBERMETZ in reserve to Portuguese troops. Motor Lorry conveyed stores and blankets. Weather good.	AD/W.
ROBERMETZ and DOULIEU (F.30.C.3.5.)	9th.	3.30am	Enemy opened heavy bombardment along whole front. Back areas, railways and roads being shelled with H.V. guns and H.E. by artillery side with howitzers at 8am notice of Enemy's strong and determined attack on Portuguese troops. Enemy launched strong and determined attack on Portuguese troops towards MADRINO. 5 Officers moved forward with fighting limbers. Two sections went forward and took up positions established in shell holes about G.24.b. on the W.b.R of the river LYS. These guns covered the bridge crossing the river LYS at about G.16.c.4.6. which had been left intact. Excellent targets were obtained on enemy formations attempting to cross the bridge and severe casualties were inflicted on him. Despite the enemy's determined attacks, he was held in check until dark. During darkness harassing fire was maintained on SAILLY-SUR-LA-LYS and roads leading there. Casualties:- 2/9Ranks wounded. Nos. 3 & 4 Sections took up reserve positions about L.14.d.5.9. and co-operated in harassing fire during darkness. Meanwhile M.T. transport formed transport of 1st 50th Inf. Bde. at DOULIEU (F.30.C.3.5.) Rations in reserve were sent up to from DOULIEU at 4pm. Weather good.	AD/W.
GOÉMARQUETTE FARM. E.Y.a.O.8 (36a/40,000)	10th.	4.30am	During the night the enemy had succeeded in obtaining a footing on the W. bank of the river LYS. Hostile M.G. and rifle fire was very intense and his artillery which had moved forward during the night shelled our new line and back area. The enemy's artillery paid most attention to back areas, using a Y.M. and M.G. barrage on our front system. In event of recent situation on the SOMME the absence of aerial contact during this operation is worthy of note. Hostile formations approaching the river were quite visible during the day, and observation shewed that casualties among the enemy were very severe. General bombardment at the bridge at G.16.C.4.6. One section alone fired 35,000 rounds. Casualties:- 6/9Ranks wounded. 2/9Ranks bombed and 2/9Ranks missing.	AD/W.

WAR DIARY

"B" COMPANY.   **50th Bn. MACHINE GUN CORPS.**   Army Form C. 2118.

VOLUME 24.   **SHEET 3.**   **APRIL. 1918.**

INTELLIGENCE SUMMARY. REF. SHEETS. 36a and 36a/NW,000

Place	Date APRIL	Hour	Summary of Events and Information	Remarks and references to Appendices
GDE MARQUETTE FARM. E.4.a.O.8. (36a/NW,000)	10TH (cont.)		Transport moved to F.7.26.d.2.9. at 9.30am arriving there at 11am, and again moved at 6.30pm to GDE MARQUETTE FARM. (See marginal ref.) Weather good. 2 horses Stationo sent up line at 5.30pm. Rations Coy. joined Transport from Adv. Coy. H.Q.	WB n.
"	11TH	7.30am	During the morning the Infantry withdrew their line, and the guns of Nos 1 & 2 Sections covered the withdrawal. Enemy again attacked at about 4.30 a.m, but he was held in check until the new line of defence was established, 1000 rounds were fired by one section at ranges varying from 100 to 200 yards with excellent results. On completion of the withdrawal the guns fell back to about QUENNELLE FARM, where new positions were established. Transport standing as yesterday. Casualties Offrs: (Acting Lt. JENNER (M.C.) wounded to base. 9th R. Reid. 9th Ranks wounded 2 9th Ranks missing. 39th R. Reid. 9th Ranks missing	WB n.
MORBECQUE	12th.		3 Sections relieved through YEUX BEQUIN and took up battle positions in the neighbourhood of LAMOTTE where a support line was established. The remaining Section covered the withdrawal of the line and did excellent work, inflicting severe casualties on the advancing enemy. General Woollcombe Mr. Penno were engaged and silenced. During the afternoon several of our aeroplanes dropped bombs on enemy formations. Transport moved to MORBECQUE at 6.15am, arriving there at 2.30pm. Casualties:- 29th Ranks wounded. 39th R. missing.	WB n.
CHIENNES	13th.		Advanced Coy. H.Q. established at LAMOTTE, in present Consolidation of support line in front of LAMOTTE continued. Transport standing to all day, and moved to CHIENNES at 6.15pm leaving front at 4.30 p.m. Situation shew Artillery and reinforcements appearing and enemy held in check. Weather good. Casualties nil.	WB n.
"	14th.		Transport standing fast. Coy. continued in reserve line. Enemy attack broken down by artillery fire and line remains intact. Rations sent up at 6.30pm. Weather good. Casualties nil.	WB n.

"B" COMPANY. 50th Batt. Machine Gun Corps. Army Form C. 2118.
WAR DIARY or INTELLIGENCE SUMMARY
Volume 24. Sheet 4. April 1918.

Place	Date	Hour	Summary of Events and Information	Remarks and references to Appendices
CHIENNES	15th.		Transport standing fast. Took entrained on consolidation of support line. Situation normal. Casualties - Nil. Weather dull and cold. Visibility poor.	Appx
CHIENNES and QUIESTEDE A.28.c.6.4.	16th.	8 am.	Transport moved off at 8 am and met Coys coming out of line; and Battn. proceeded to QUIESTEDE A.28.c.6.4 (Sh.36A/40,000.) Pud in Coast, acting as L.O. with "C" Coy and another officer also attached to "C" Coy. Weather good. Arrived QUIESTEDE at 8.30 pm, and remainder of day spent resting.	Appx
QUIESTEDE.	17th.		Limbers cleaned, scrubbed and oiled. Deficiencies taken and indents to complete submitted. Training commenced. Weather good.	Appx
"	18th.		Weather rough and mild. Coys inspected by Comdg. Officer at Noon. and Battn. inspected by A.O.C. at 12.15 pm. Morning spent in cleaning up equipment and personnel. Transport paraded for saluting drill at 2 pm. Usual training carried out during remainder of day.	Appx
"	19th.		Cleaning limbers during morning. Preparatory to inspection. Officers and R.Q.M.Sergts joined Coy as reinforcements. Weather good. Coys paid at 5.30 pm. Warning order received at 11.30 pm for a route Tomorrow.	Appx
QUIESTEDE and ECQUES.	20th.	9.30 am.	Coys paraded at 9.15 am. and moved off as unit transport. "C" Coy and Battn. HQ. to ECQUES S.G. i.d. 3.9. (Sheet 36A) arriving there at 12.30 pm.	Appx
ECQUES G.i.d.3.9 (Sh. 36A/40,000)	21st.		Standing by for Divine Service; but no service arranged. Weather fine.	Appx
"	22nd.		Inspection by Comdg. Officer at 9.15 am. and inspection of Coys and Transport by Battn. Comdr. at 10.30 am. Divisional fighting order, less iron rations and packs, inspected. Soft caps were worn. 30 Ranks joined Coy. as reinforcements. 40 Ranks proceeded on Pigeon Course at LIWERS. Weather cold.	Appx

O.H. Huey Lt. Col.

"B" COMPANY WAR DIARY 50TH Bn. MACHINE GUN CORPS.

or INTELLIGENCE SUMMARY.

VOLUME 24. SHEET 5 APRIL 1918.

Army Form C. 2118.

(Erase heading not required.)

Instructions regarding War Diaries and Intelligence Summaries are contained in F.S. Regs., Part II. and the Staff Manual respectively. Title pages will be prepared in manuscript.

Place	Date April	Hour	Summary of Events and Information	Remarks and references to Appendices
ECOUES. A.I.S.9. (36a/40000)	23rd.		4 Ranks under C.S.M. Henderson for P.9.5.T. at Battn. H.Q. Physical Training and usual training carried out during the day. 12 Sections bathed. Issue of small Kit by Officer Comdg: at 9.30 a.m. Weather good.	AAA w—
"	24th		Issue of clothing at 9.30 a.m. Usual training carried out during the day. Leaving Order received. Lunat party returned to Bn: H.Q. Watercart, horse and D.R. rank sent to Battn: H.Q. Weather mild.	AAA w—
"	25th		Leaving Orders, belts fitted, Limbers reported in readiness for move. Packs also placed on Limbers. Transport moved off at 11.30 a.m. and proceeded to ENIONNE RICOURT, to join 150th Infantry Group.	AAA w—
"	26th	1.30am	Coys: paraded at 1.30 a.m. in Fighting Order and met Transpt: in main fashion. Moved off in motor busses to ERIONNE RICOURT, arriving there at 9 a.m. Coy. and Transport entrained with 150th Inf: Bde: Group at 10.30 a.m. and moved off at 11.30 a.m. Weather good.	AAA w—
GRUGNY.	27th:		Travelling all day and detrained at St GILLES at 10 p.m. thence by march route to GRUGNY, a distance of about 8 km. Accommodation found into: Weather good. Transport followed Coy, arriving at GRUGNY at midnight.	AAA w—
"	28th		Cleaning guns and gun Kit, belt filling etc. Limbers cleaned and washed. Weather bad. Rain rest of the day.	AAA w—
"	29th		Usual training carried out including saluting, Physical & gun drills, mechanism and gas drill. Training programme submitted to Bn: H.Q. 2nd Rank found reinforcements	AAA w—
"	30th		Inspection of Coys: Less Transport, by O.C. at 9.30 a.m. and by Battn: Comdr. at 10.30 a.m. Disco: Fed: March: 5 Order and Drill A.C.I. 64/03. Usual training. 2nd Rank found fatigues. Remaining recites H.Q. Ranks found reinforcements on instruction in P.9.S.T.	AAA w—

O.C. "B" Machine Gun Coy. *[signature]* Captain

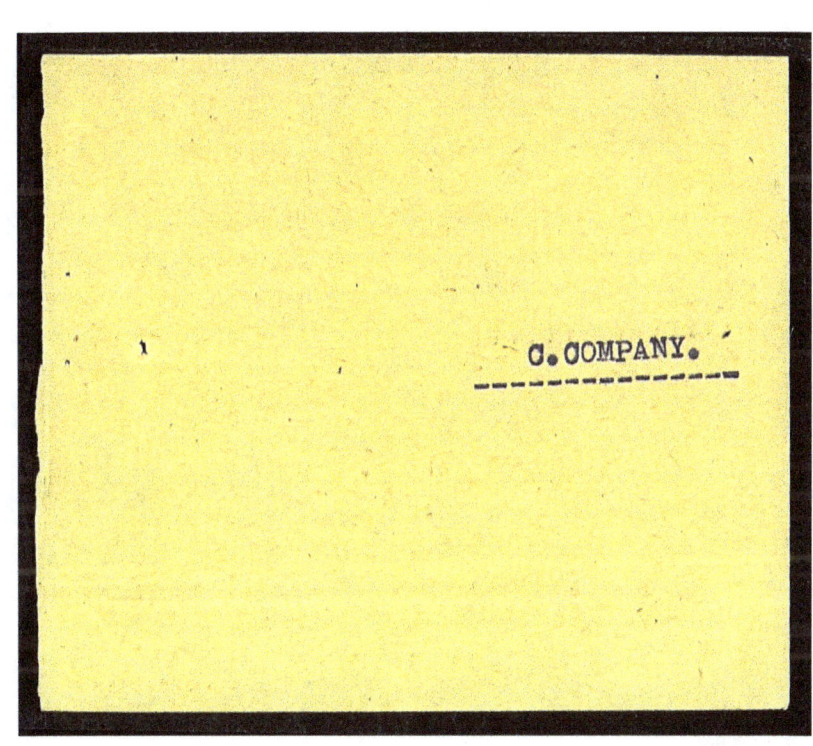

Army Form C. 2118.

WAR DIARY
or
INTELLIGENCE SUMMARY.

C "Coy" 150th Batn.
M.G. Corps.

(Erase heading not required.)

Instructions regarding War Diaries and Intelligence Summaries are contained in F. S. Regs., Part II. and the Staff Manual respectively. Title pages will be prepared in manuscript.

Place	Date	Hour	Summary of Events and Information	Remarks and references to Appendices
	APRIL 1918.			
	1.		Company (less Transport and party with Capt Ralston in the line) entrained at SALEUX about 9am; detrained at ROE (1pm) and marched to ARGUES arriving about 3pm. Capt Ralstons party (including 2/Lt Bulbis & Graham and about 30 O.R.) were in action South of the Somme. Some machine guns were heavily engaged during the morning assisting a counter attack on the wood South of HANGARD which was successful. Enemy shelled all day especially in various Donmart. One Shell fell on HQrs killing 2 O.R. About 6pm the guns were relieved and whole personnel proceeded in small parties to GENTELLES. After a short halt they proceeded to LONGUEAU arriving about 3am (2nd) Transport (which had journeyed by road) arrived at ARGUES in the afternoon.	Rln
	2		Capt Ralston and party marched to SALEUX and entrained 9pm	Rln
	3		Detrained at ROE at 7.30 am — tea was served — marched to ARGUES and there joined the remainder of the Company. Reinforcements — 33 O.R. (including 1 Sergeant & 2 Corporals) arrived. Warning order to move to new position.	Rln
	4		Transport started on the journey by road. The Division moved to 1st Army area. Company marched to DOURIEZ, journeyed by bus to near BUSNES (via HESDIN, St. POL, LILLERS) and marched to billets in TOBECQ arriving about 6.30 pm.	MKenleyr Rln

WAR DIARY or INTELLIGENCE SUMMARY

Army Form C. 2118.

"C" Bath 50 Batt. M.G. Corps

Place	Date	Hour	Summary of Events and Information	Remarks and references to Appendices
ROBECQ	April 1918		At ROBECQ	
	6		Transport arrived at Mt BERNENCHON. Horses, mules & harness remained in billets there. Limbers were brought to ROBECQ.	Rlm
	7		Lt A.M. Jones, M.C. — transferred to "A" Coy as O.C. 2Lt L.R. Butlin M.C. — acting 2 in Command 2Lt N.N.L. Harrison — transferred from 17 Coy as 7O	Rlm
	8		Proceeded by march route to billets between MERVILLE and ESTAIRES (about L26d., L32 h.) (Sheet 36A)	Rlm
	9		There was a very heavy bombardment during the night and it transpires that the enemy had made an attack on the PORTUGUESE. At 8 am warning order was received to be ready to move as 1 hours notice. About 1.30 Lt L.C. Tomlinson (F.I.P. Landel with No 11 Section a LA BREQUE with No 10 Section set out for LA GORGUE to report to O/C "D" Company owing to horses collapsing in LA GORGUE guns the had to be manhandled to their positions. The 4 guns of No 10 Section (Lt Landel) took up positions on railway South of Estaires between R4 d.0.8 and L35 c.2.8 (Sheet 36A). Two guns under Lt Tomlinson were placed in trenches at PONT RIQUEL (R10 d.2.8) and two guns under Lt Landel at LESTREM Lock (R9 c.2.0)	Rlm

A.5834 Wt. W4973/M687 750,000 8/16 D.D. & L. Ltd. Forms/C.2118/13

Ref: map - 36A.

WAR DIARY
or
INTELLIGENCE SUMMARY.

Army Form C. 2118.

"C" Coy
50 Battn
M.G. Corps

Place	Date	Hour	Summary of Events and Information	Remarks and references to Appendices
	APRIL 1918		From these positions good targets were engaged. Heavy losses inflicted on the enemy. The 4 guns of No 10 Section withdrew at night to positions in LESTREM. Coy HQ with the remaining teams moved to a farm in L.12.c. Transport moved back to about K.13.c.2.2. (East of Bois Morgan).	
	10.		About 2 am the enemy attacked, working round the right flank. Lt Tomlinson had to withdraw with one gun (the other having both gun and 3 actions) He moved his men back to Q.4.c.9.6. and himself went to Transport Lines for ammunition & rations. In the morning the guns of No 12 Section took up positions on the left of Bois Bayard and those of No 9 Section on East of LESTREM. No 9 Section's guns gave support to the infantry in a counter attack and also held up an enemy attack for some considerable time. Eventually the guns of No 9 & 12 Sections had to withdraw and did so fighting a rearguard action along with the infantry. No 10 Section guns about 9am withdrew to a line between LESTREM & LESTR.REF, along the railway. Transport moved to F.29 central.	RRM
	11.		Capt. Ralston acting O/C 9/4 East Yorks. Lt Tomlinson with his one remaining gun and one gun of D Coy	

Ref: map - Sheet 3619.

Army Form C. 2118.

WAR DIARY C Coy
or 30 Bn
INTELLIGENCE SUMMARY. M.G. Corps

(Erase heading not required.)

Instructions regarding War Diaries and Intelligence
Summaries are contained in F. S. Regs., Part II.
and the Staff Manual respectively. Title pages
will be prepared in manuscript.

Place	Date	Hour	Summary of Events and Information	Remarks and references to Appendices
	APRIL 1918			
	12.		Took up position in L.31.d. - An enemy battalion appeared in EPINETTE and was engaged with good effect. Other parties were engaged until the situation on the left made it necessary to withdraw to North side of the canal. Guns under L/S Johnson & Lander were put places in a farm at L.31.c.O.8. covering light railway tracks. The Lewis guns withdrew & then guns moved to K.30.d. The left flank gave way suddenly and one gun was lost in retiring - these men now returned to transport lines. No.10 Section guns which had positions in the vicinity of LESTREM Station were also forced to withdraw & returned to transport lines. Guns of Section 9 v 12 fought a rearguard action transport - with B v C Sections - moved by night to D.23.d.	Rbh.
	13.		Two composite teams were formed and took up position to cover the right flank of 149 Inf. Bde. After withdrawing there were relieved by guns of 32 Bn M.G.C. Coy H.Q. which had been established at VIEUX BERQUIN moved during the evening the guns having been relieved and withdrawn to reserve positions. Transport moved at 5 a.m. to BLENSECQUE. Coy moved back to V.9.d, I was billeted in farms.	Rbh. C M Mun W M

Army Form C. 2118.

C Coy.
35th Bn
M.G. Corps.

WAR DIARY
or
INTELLIGENCE SUMMARY.
(Erase heading not required.)

Place	Date	Hour	Summary of Events and Information	Remarks and references to Appendices
IN THE FIELD	14		APRIL 1918. Four gun teams moved up to occupy reserve position. These returned to Billets at night. Capt Ralston returned.	Rbn.
	15		Positions were again taken up during the day and one gun was mounted at HQrs for A.A. work. These returned at night.	Rbn.
	16.		Company moved back to transport lines & whole Company moved to COCHENDAL. Capt Ralston attached to Battn HQ as 2nd i/c. Lt R.C. Moon - transferred from B Coy - O.C.	Rbn.
	16-19		2Lt W.M. Gray — do — attached to D Coy.	Rbn.
	"		Lt L.C. Tomlinson " " " 19 Coy.	Rbn.
	16. 20.		Lt J.R. Graham	Rbn.
	18.		Company in Billets at COCHENDAL.	Rbn.
	19		Inspection by G.O.C. (Division). Reinforcements - 3 officers (Lt J. Morrison, Lt H.W. Needham and 2Lt G.C. Holcroft) and 19 men arrived.	Rbn.
	20.		Company marched to ECQUES.	Rbn.
	20. 6. 25.		Coy. in Billets at ECQUES.	Althoughn? Rbn.

Army Form C. 2118.

WAR DIARY
or
INTELLIGENCE SUMMARY.

(Erase heading not required.)

C Coy
50 Bn.
M.G. Corps

Instructions regarding War Diaries and Intelligence Summaries are contained in F. S. Regs., Part II. and the Staff Manual respectively. Title pages will be prepared in manuscript.

Place	Date	Hour	Summary of Events and Information	Remarks and references to Appendices
			April 1918	
			Casualties :-	
	1		2 OR Killed	
	10		1 OR Killed	
			5 OR wounded	
			2/Lt J. Butler & 7th N.Z. Maddocks wounded	
	11		9 OR wounded	
			G.R.A. Farrell wounded	
	12		Previously wounded (died of wounds)	
			1 OR Killed	
			7 OR wounded	
			2 OR missing	

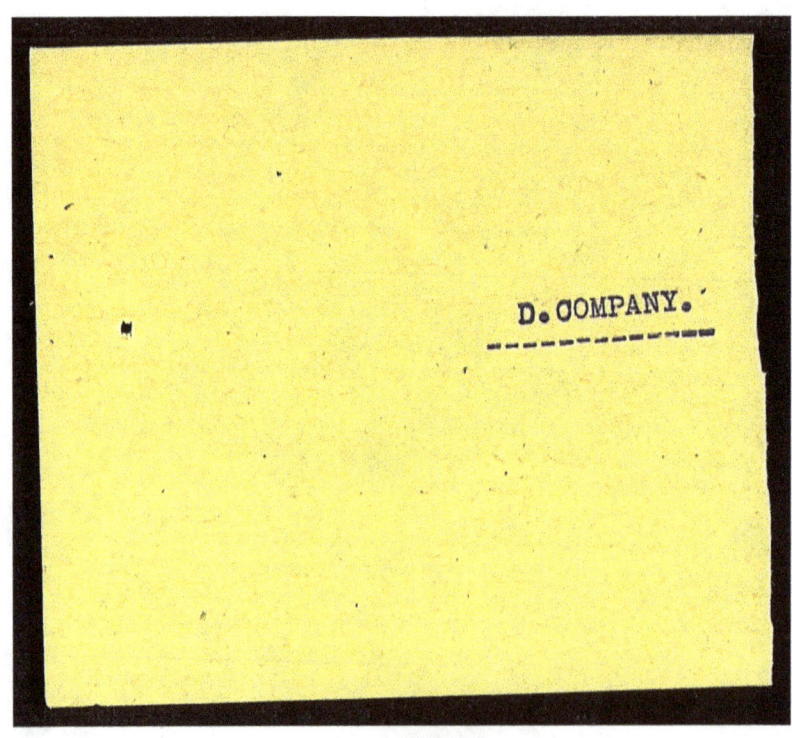

Army Form C. 2118.

WAR DIARY
or
INTELLIGENCE SUMMARY.
(Erase heading not required.)

Instructions regarding War Diaries and Intelligence Summaries are contained in F. S. Regs., Part II and the Staff Manual respectively. Title pages will be prepared in manuscript.

Place	Date	Hour	Summary of Events and Information	Remarks and references to Appendices
ROBECQ 14f.r sheet 36A 1/40,000	7:4:18		2/Lt. M.B. Douglas joined Company as acting 2nd in Command. – Company billetted in area P.28.a.	No orders for this move received among the Company documents.
	8:4:18		The Company moved by road to CHAPELLE DUVELLE & billetted about L.27.c.0.7.	
ESTAIRES	9:4:18	9 a.m.	The company moved off to take up positions in front of ESTAIRES No. I Section in vicinity of Railway (2/Lt Beele PARSONS) " II " " " " PONT ROCHON (LIEUT BALBI) " III " " " Pont RIPOUL (2/Lt DERBYSHIRE & 2/Lt LEE) " IV " " " at Pont, L29.B.3 at bridge trench about L.29.B.3.3. No. V Section in reserve trench about L.29.6.7. (2/Lt TEAGUE).	Standing orders or instructions used in the occasion of Capt. W.R.T.Lemann (see later).
			No. I Section in reserve remained at L.29.6.7. 2/Lt. DERBYSHIRE was wounded while moving up into positions.	
		5 p.m.	2/Lt TEAGUE sent his gun to take up a position at PONT LEVIS.	
		6.00pm	Received verbal orders from Bde. H.Q. to take remaining 2 guns & cover the Railway Bridge - cross the RIVER LAWE at R.2.7.95.99 & a gap in the infantry line at L.33.	
			Bde. H.Q. then moved to AVIATION GROUND L.32.a.7.7. where Company Headquarters were also established early in the following morning.	
AVIATION GROUND L.32.a.7.7.	10:4:18		Company Headquarters remained at AVIATION GROUND.	
ROBERMETZ.	11:4:18	11 a.m.	Company Headquarters moved to ROBERMETZ. (K.24.3.6.). About 6 p.m. Company Headquarters including Capt. W.R. Lemann, Capt. M.B. Douglas & Lt. GRAVES were relieved by Portugese Major 150th Infantry Bde. to join the infantry Line along keeps in night of road leading to NEUF BERQUIN. Capt. THOMSON was taken prisoner & Lt. GRAVES wounded.	

Wt. w12839/M1291 750,000. 1/17. D. D. & L., Ltd. Forms/C2118/14.

Army Form C. 2118.

WAR DIARY
INTELLIGENCE SUMMARY.
(Erase heading not required.)

Instructions regarding War Diaries and Intelligence Summaries are contained in F. S. Regs., Part II. and the Staff Manual respectively. Title pages will be prepared in manuscript.

Place	Date	Hour	Summary of Events and Information	Remarks and references to Appendices
11.c.	11.4.18		Company Headquarters established for the night at K 15 c 6.5. Transport at E 20 central.	
	12.4.18		Company Headquarters moved to K 14 d 2.6. & personnel that in the firing line with infantry.	
		2 p.m.	LIEUT GRAHAM C Coy. 50th Batt. M.G.C. reported with 2 guns & with one gun belonging to this Coy. was sent to take up a position at LES LAURIERS (K.14.d.) & cover the road to MERVILLE. Further orders taken up at K.14.d.9070 and on the Chateau at K15 c 00.15. & meantime been posted were and aged. 2/LT LENNHTON of the 57th Batt. M.G.C. who turned including a field gun then engaged, joined the Section at LES LAURIERS had been attacked to the infantry. S.A.A. to this section — received 6.30 p.m.	App. I.
		6.30 p.m.	Arrangements were made to get 19,000 nds. S.A.A. to this section — received 6.30 p.m.	
		7.45 p.m.	Orders for relief were received from the 150th M. Tde. at 7.45 p.m. Moved to LA MOTTE CHATEAU (D.30.c)	
LA MOTTE CHATEAU	13.4.18		Received verbal orders from Capt. 57th Batt. M.G.C. to move to area J.3.c. — Moved off early & quartered personnel in farm at J.3.c.2.0. Received orders from Bgt. to reorganise company in the house of 4 sections, each comprising 2 guns & ammunition & 4 gun teams when action when guns personnel & S.A.A. were available.	App. II.
	14.4.18		Received orders from O.C. 67 & 13th Batt M.G.C. each respect to duties in case of alarm.	App. III.
	15.4.18		Under instructed from O.C. 60 & 73 Batt M.G.C. officers were allotted to the Company as follows:— CAPT. M.B. DOUGLAS (Acting B.D.) LIEUT TOMLINSON (Acting 2nd i/c) 2/LIEUT SEARANEKE (Transport Officer) 2/LT TEAGUE. 2/LT PEARSON.	App. IV.

WAR DIARY or INTELLIGENCE SUMMARY

Army Form C. 2118.

Instructions regarding War Diaries and Intelligence Summaries are contained in F. S. Regs., Part II. and the Staff Manual respectively. Title pages will be prepared in manuscript.

(Erase heading not required.)

Place	Date	Hour	Summary of Events and Information	Remarks and references to Appendices
	15:4:18		Casualties since 9:4:18 — Officers:- Wounded 2/Lt DERBYSHIRE 2/Lt PARSONS Lt GRAVES. Missing CAPT W.R. THOMSON. LIEUT BALBI 2/Lt LEE Other Ranks: Killed — 5 Wounded — 17 Missing — 46	
G^t QUIESTEDE	16:4:18		Moved to G^t QUIESTEDE. 50th Divisional Warning Order No. 197 & 50th Division Operation Order No. 198. Company billeted in area A30.7.	App. V + VI
	24:4:18		Nos. 13, 15 + 16 Sections with Coy. Wagon moved to CHATEAU LAPREYLE.	
	25:4:18		Received 50th Div. Warning Order No. 200	App. VII
			Received 50th Div. Operation Order No. 201	App. VIII
			Received 50th Div. Administration Instruction No. 45	App. IX
	26:4:18		Received 151st Bde. Operation Order No. 160 & Administration Instruction. Received Council for constructing from Belgn. 50th Bn^d. M.G.C. Transport Officer. Company Operation Order No. 1A.	App. X App. XI
	26:4:18	6.30pm	Marched out of G^t QUIESTEDE to embusing point H10 B 0.6 (about S of Church in WITTES)	
LAPUGNOY	27:4:18	3.30am	Left LAPUGNOY Station.	
CRUGNY	28:4:18	6pm	Arrived CRUGNY — men billeted in billets — officers billeted in the village.	

Malcolm B. Douglas
OC "D" Coy 50th Batt. M.G.C.

Volume II

Confidential

War Diary
of
50th/99 Batt. M.G.C.

From May 1st 1918
To   May 31st 1918.

Army Form C. 2118.

WAR DIARY
or
INTELLIGENCE SUMMARY.
(Erase heading not required.)

Instructions regarding War Diaries and Intelligence Summaries are contained in F. S. Regs., Part II. and the Staff Manual respectively. Title pages will be prepared in manuscript.

Place	Date	Hour	Summary of Events and Information	Remarks and references to Appendices
CRUGNY	1st		Battalion at rest. Tactical exercise carried out under Divisional arrangements. Lt. Col. C.H. Hoare also up.Col. for Lt.Col. m. Command of the Bn.	Bty.
	2nd		Battalion at rest. Training carried out under Company arrangements.	Astin
	3rd		Battalion at rest. Training carried out under Company arrangements.	Astin
	4th		Battalion at rest. Training carried out under Company arrangements.	Astin
MERVAL	5th		Battalion moved to MERVAL by march route in accordance with O.O. No. 1. and arrived at 12.30 p.m. C.O. and Coy. Commanders visited the forward area in the afternoon.	Astin Appendix I
	6th		Battalion at rest. Training carried out under Company arrangements. C.O., 2nd in command, & Coy. Commanders reconnoitred the line. 2nd Lieut. G.W.E. PEEL and Lieut. B.B. JACK with 119.O.R.'s IX Corps Cyclist Battn reported for duty.	Bty.
	7th		Battalion preparing for the line. C.O. visited forward area. A, B, and D coys. relieved French Inf. G. coys in accordance with 51st (French) Div. Order No. 503 and C.O's verbal instructions.	Astin
In the line	8th		C.O. assumed command of the machine guns on divisional front at 8 a.m.	Appendix II Bty.

Opt. 1. lr.

Army Form C. 2118.

WAR DIARY
or
INTELLIGENCE SUMMARY.
(Erase heading not required.)

Instructions regarding War Diaries and Intelligence Summaries are contained in F. S. Regs., Part II. and the Staff Manual respectively. Title pages will be prepared in manuscript.

Place	Date	Hour	Summary of Events and Information	Remarks and references to Appendices
In the line	8th		C coy. relieved French Machine Guns in accordance with 51st (French) Div. Order No. 503 and C.O.'s verbal instructions. Batt. H.Q. established at le Calvaire PONTAVERT.	Appx.
	9th		Situation very quiet. C.O. sited M.G. emplacements and conferred with G.O.C. 50th Div. and Corps M.G.O. about scheme of M.G. defence.	Appx.
	10th		Situation unchanged. C.O. attended conference at 151st I.B.H.Q. and reconnoitred "C" coy sector. Casualties:- 1 O.R. accidentally wounded of "B" coy.	Appx.
	11th		Slight increase of enemy artillery activity noticeable. On night 11th/12th two St. Etienne guns took up positions in intermediate line relieving four Vickers guns of "A" Coy. & four of "C" Coy. which were withdrawn to their support lines at MAIZY. These positions were previously garrisoned by C.O.	Appx.
	12th		Six guns of "D" coy were relieved by St. Etienne guns, and one by Vickers guns of "B" Coy, which were moved forward. "D" Coy was withdrawn to MA.12.Y and held in tactical reserve. Afterwards another St. Etienne guns took up positions in intermediate line. Situation quiet and unchanged. Batt. H.Q. moved from P.C. CALVAIRE and were established at BEAURIEUX at 10 p.m.	Appx.

CHA y Ch

Army Form C. 2118.

WAR DIARY
or
INTELLIGENCE SUMMARY.
(Erase heading not required.)

Instructions regarding War Diaries and Intelligence Summaries are contained in F. S. Regs., Part II. and the Staff Manual respectively. Title pages will be prepared in manuscript.

Place	Date	Hour	Summary of Events and Information	Remarks and references to Appendices
In the line.	13.		Slightly increased enemy artillery activity on back area otherwise situation quiet and unchanged. Relief and changes of gun positions carried out in accordance with Batt. Orders No. 3	Army
	14.		Situation unchanged. E.O. sited 10 emplacements on a reserve line of defence and reconnoitred 'bus line. At 10.30 p.m. hostile aircraft bombed our	Appendix 3 Army
	15.		BEAURIEUX. Further reconnaissance of reserve line of defence by E.O. and Major M.B. DOUGLAS. Situation unchanged. Major V.B.J. SAXON IX Corps Cyclist Batt. reported for duty and assumed command of IX Corps Cyclist Detachment. The E.O. conferred with O's Cmdg Companies	Army.
	16.		Unchanged. E.O. conferred with Coys to H.Q.	Army
	17.		E.O. visited line with E.R.E. O.C. "D" Coy with view to officers reconnoitred defence line. 1 St. Etienne gun withdrawn for instructional purposes.	Army
	18.		Coy commanders' conference. Demonstration of St. Etienne gun to G.S. S.O.2 Div. E.O. attended G.O.C.'s conference. Tactical exercise carried out by "D" Coy. during night 18./19.	Army

Army Form C. 2118.

WAR DIARY
or
INTELLIGENCE SUMMARY.
(Erase heading not required.)

Instructions regarding War Diaries and Intelligence Summaries are contained in F. S. Regs., Part II. and the Staff Manual respectively. Title pages will be prepared in manuscript.

Place	Date	Hour	Summary of Events and Information	Remarks and references to Appendices
In the line	19th		Hostile Artillery active throughout the day. Great activity of enemy aircraft over trench. Great Coy. at 1-30 AM covering party of N.F. came in contact with enemy patrol, we took two prisoners, two of our men missing	
	20th		Artillery activity normal. A hostile machine was observed flying very low and apparently taking photos. The markings of the machine was different to the usual used, even it had a good black cross enclosed in a white ring	
	21st		Artillery activity mostly confined to counter battery work. Great activity during night. Our enemy lines organization to be visibly. Battn to BEAURISNX relieved CO's conference. Hostile Artillery less active than harassing	offensive opn
	22		fire by enemy h.g's during night	
	23		Harassing fire by enemy h.g's during the night. At 2-45 Artillery duel opened on our right and lasting until 3 a.e. Heavy M.G. observed firing from corner of ZIG ZAG WOOD	
	24		Arnl active normal. Artillery activity normal. At 9-15 PM demonstration barrage by our artillery lasting two minutes On the night of the 24th 12 St Etienne guns were relieved by 12 Vickers Guns.	C.M. Potter

WAR DIARY
or
INTELLIGENCE SUMMARY.
(Erase heading not required.)

Army Form C. 2118.

Place	Date	Hour	Summary of Events and Information	Remarks and references to Appendices
In the line	24th		CONTINUED	
			at 1 am	
			A raid was carried out by the left Brigade which was repulsed by	OH
			S.A. fire. 3.25 am 100 rds were fired on all the front line brought	
			in all machine guns fired well. The infantry reported that the	
			machine gun barrage was very effective.	
	25		Artillery exceedingly quiet. Aerial activity normal. 3 Coy relieved	OH
			B Coy. A raid was carried out by the centre Brigade, one prisoner was captured. All vehicle M guns indicated Appendix 5	
	26		opened. Conference at 4.30. At 5.30 pm orders received to "STAND TO"	MH
			at 9.15 pm orders received to "Move to ASSEMBLY POSITIONS". The reserve	
			Company immediately moved to ASSEMBLY positions at P.C. TERRASSE	
			Sections in reserve were moved up to their respective companies	
			An additional Lewis Gun was sent to A Coy and Gun to C Coy. Heavy rain during	
27-29			At 1 am 27th a very heavy bombardment was commenced on the whole Corps	MH
			front followed by an attack in great strength	a Memdix 6
	29		At 3.30 pm orders received at Brigade Argonne to report down at	MH
			GUY LE JARD. C.O. rode on to make necessary arrangements	
			Battalion left at 2.30 am arriving at 2.30 am 30th	

CHH MCR

Army Form C. 2118.

WAR DIARY
or
INTELLIGENCE SUMMARY.
(Erase heading not required.)

Instructions regarding War Diaries and Intelligence Summaries are contained in F. S. Regs., Part II. and the Staff Manual respectively. Title pages will be prepared in manuscript.

Place	Date	Hour	Summary of Events and Information	Remarks and references to Appendices
S.H. Cne	30th		Orders received at 11am to move to BRÉOIL. At 2.30pm on arrival further orders received to move on to SUZY arriving at 7.30pm. No billets were available and the battalion bivouacked in perfect weather on the edge of a wood outside the village.	O.N.
	31st		Orders received to move to CONAY – Cantonment area – notified. Subsequently to CONAY – FRICBRUNGES area and then whilst on the line of march to CONAY the Commanding officer went on to arrange billets. The battalion and B details of M.G.C. of 149 Bt. arr. at CONAY. Owing to a mistake in interpretation of a verbal order the Battalion were in FERBRANGES where nothing had been arranged & which was already full of other transports and artillery. There was no available ground on which to bivouack & eventually officers and men were crowded into barns. Nine small rooms.	O.N. Off. + per.

SECRET.

CORRIGENDA No. 1   Copy No. 13.
to

Organization of 50th. Bn., M.G.C., in the

BEAURIEUX Sector.
- - - - - - - - - - - - -

AMMUNITION Para.   In last line substitute for Paragraph No. 4,
SUPPLY.   5.   Paragraph No. 3.

MESSAGES   Para.   (a).   The runner will be sent to P. C.
AND   9.   CALVAIRE and hand over messages to
REPORTS.   an orderly from Battn., H.Q..

                                    [signature] Capt., & Adj.,
22nd. May, 1918.   50th. Bn., M.G.C..

Copies to. :-

    (1). - Commanding Officer.
    (2). - O.C., Signal Section.
    (3). - Quartermaster.
    (4). - O.C., A Coy..
    (5). -   "   B "
    (6). -   "   C "
    (7). -   "   D "
    (8). - 149th. Inf. Bde..
    (9). - 150th. Inf. Bde..
    (10). - 151st. Inf. Bde..
    (11). - 50th. Div., - G..
    (12). - War Diary.
    (13). -   "   "
    (14). - File.

APPENDIX I

50th BATTN. MACHINE GUN CORPS.   Copy No 5

OPERATION ORDER NO 1.

1.   Reference 50th Divisional Operation Order No 202 and March Table
The Battalion will be at the road junction N.W. of CRUGNY facing N.E. at 8.30 a.m. 5th instant in the following order:-
Head-Quarters; "A","B", "C", & "D" Coys.
Coy. Transports will move in rear of their respective Companies.

2.   2 lorries have been detailed to report at these Head-quarters at 12.0 noon, which will be alloted as follows:-

    1 lorry Battn. H.Q's.
    1 lorry, between 4 Companies, (to carry blankets only.)

Blankets will be rolled in bundles of 20 10, labelled, and stacked outside Battalion Q.M.Stores before moving.
Officer Comdg. "B" Coy. will detail SIX O.R's as loading party to report to R.Q.M.S. at 8.15 a.m.
The R.Q.M.S. will be responsible for the loading of both lorries.

3.   Coy. Commanders may carry their mens' packs on their transport if accomodation is available.

Acknowledge.

Copies:- 1. "A" Coy.
        2. "B" Coy.
        3. "C" Coy.
        4. "D" Coy.
        5. File.
        6. War Diary.

                                      Capt. & Adjt.
                                  50th Battn. M.G. Corps.

4-5-18.

/'38° CORPS D'ARMEE.   SECRET.
51° DIVISION.

GENERAL STAFF.   Copy No. 10.

                 TRANSLATION.
No. 503.   H.Q., 5-5-1918.

OPERATION ORDER.

(Relief og the 51st. (French) Division by
the 50th. (British) Division.).

----

1. The 51st. (French) Division, will be relieved by the 50th. (British) Division.
   The relief will commence on the night of the 6th./7th. and will be completed by the morning of the 10th. May, 1918.

2. --

MACHINE GUNS.

The Machine Gun Companies of the French Battalions of the 51st. (French) Division in the line will be relieved by the 50th. (British) Battalion, Machine Gun Corps as under. :-

        Right Sub-Sector   -   "A" Company.
        Centre   "   -   "B"   "
        Left   "   -   "C" & "D" Coys..
(A British Machine Gun Company consists of 16 Guns).

The localities of the British Machine Gun Companies will be arranged by the O/C., 50th. British Machine Gun Battalion, and the Machine Gun Captain of the 51st. (French) Division.

----

3. <u>Details of the Relief.</u> - Necessary movements to carry out the relief are detailed in the attached table.

Operation Order, No. 503, contd., - 2.

4. ------------------------------
   ----

5. ------------------------------
   ----

6. ------------------------------
   ----

7. ------------------------------

   The Machine Gun Companies of the First Line Battalions of the 51st. (French) Division, will remain in action for twenty-four hours after the relief of their Battalions. On the expiration of these periods all such detachments will rejoin their Units direct in their new locations.

                    (Signed)   Le Général BOULANGÉ
                                        Commandant,
   P.A. Le Chef   la 51° Division D'Infanterie.
       d'etat. Major.
                             Signé   BOULANGÉ.
  (Signed) R. DENTZ.

--------------- oooooo ---------------

Appendix 2.

51° DIVISION.

Etat-Major.
3è Bureau.

No 503.

MARCH TABLE.

RELIEF OF THE 51st. (FRENCH) DIVISION INFANTERIE BY THE 50th. (BRITISH) INFANTRY DIVISION.

Units of the 50th. (British) Division.	Relieve.	During the Night of.	Crossing the River Aine at the following Bridges.	Route.	Relieved Units will go to.	Route.
50th. Battalion; "A" Coy.	------	------	PONTAVERT: Bridge. 13 Bis.. 9.30 p.m..	PONTAVERT – BUTTE de L'EDMOND.		
" B "	------	------	CONCEVREUX: Bridge. 17. 8.30 p.m..	CHAUDARDES – Carriere Centrale – Ferme du TEMPLE.		
" C "	------	------	MAIZY: Bridge. 19. 8.30 p.m..	BEAURIEUX – CRAONNELLE – CRAONNE.		
" D "	------	------	– ditto. –	– ditto. –		
Machine Gun Corps.	------	oooooo				

Ref. Map :-
BERRY-AU-BAC N.O.) 1/10,000.
CHEMIN des DAMES N.E.)
and Sketch Map attached.

APPENDIX IV

SECRET.

Copy No. 4.

ORGANIZATION OF THE 50th. M.G. Bn.,
IN THE BEAURIEUX SECTOR.

POSITIONS OF GUNS. (1). There are at present forty Vickers guns in line, and twenty four guns in reserve.
In addition to this twenty six St. Etienne guns, manned by infantry personnel, are in support positions.
Sketch Map attached.

ATTACK ORDERS. (2). On receipt of the order "STAND TO" :-
The Coy. in Divisional reserve and the two reserve sections will at once load fighting limbers and will be prepared to move at fifteen minutes notice after the order "MOVE TO ASSEMBLY POSITIONS" has been received.
On receipt of this order :-
(1). Right and centre reserve sections will move via the BEAURIEUX - PONTAVERT road to CENTRE D'EVREUX and will come under the orders of their respective O.C.'s for employment as ordered by the B.G.C. their respective sub sections.
(2). The Reserve Coy. will move to a position of assembly in the neighbourhood of P.C. TERRASSE. This position together with a site for Coy. H.Q. whence telephone communication can be readily established with Divisional H.Q. will be reconnoitred by O.C., D. Coy. and a report will be rendered by noon May 25th. Each Coy. as it comes into reserve will reconnoitre the intermediate line from LA HUTTE inclusive to the Left Divisional Boundary, and also the spur running between OULCHES and CRAONNELLE in order to become familiar with the ground. A road, alternative to the BEAURIEUX - CRAONNELLE road, will be reconnoitred for use in case that road is heavily shelled.
(3). Two petrol tins of water per gun will be stored in each of the ten emplacements on the BEAURIEUX - LE BLANC SABLON CH. line. Four bicycles will be handed over to O.C., Reserve Coy. on the order "STAND TO".
Gun emplacements for the right reserve section have already been constructed near the BUTTE DE L'EDMOND, and alternative positions for the centre reserve sections are in course of construction in TR. DARCY, BOYAU GINESTEY, and the line of redoubts OUV. DES PINS - OUV. & CORNE.
(4). Officers - Commanders of Coys. in the line will at once report to H.Q. Bdes. in whose sub sections they are operating.
2nd. i/c. Coys. will once proceed to Battle H.Q..
Two Officers of each Coy. in addition to the T.O. will remain at wagon lines.

(1).

TANKS. (3). In the event of an attack by Tanks, gun teams will remember that their primary duty is to annihilate the infantry following the tanks, the destruction of the tanks themselves being of minor importance.

On this front it is evident that the co-operation of tanks in any attack is controlled by the belt of woodland extending along the whole of the divisional sector, in rear of the redoubt line, and that deep penetration is only possible via the BUTTE DE L'EDMOND and PONTAVERT.

Gun emplacements in the neighbourhood of the BUTTE DE L'EDMOND occupied or prepared for occupation by the reserve section will be stocked with 500 rounds of armour piercing S.A.A. per emplacement - i.e. 4,000 rounds in all - as also Nos: 1 & 2 reserve emplacements on the slopes west of BEAURIEUX - i.e. - 1,000 rounds.

The remainder of the armour piercing S.A.A. will be distributed as follows :-

(a) Forward Guns -
Nos: 1, 2 & 5 - each 250 rounds.

(b) Support Guns -
No. 9 - - - - 250 rounds.

FIRE CONTROL. (4). Forward guns will in no case fire more than six belts and rear guns not more than eight belts on their S.O.S. lines.

Subject to this order all guns will open on their S.O.S. lines as soon as an S.O.S. is observed on the front they cover.

AMMUNITION SUPPLY. (5). The following supply of ammunition will be maintained. :-

At each gun emplacement 16 belt boxes and 2,000 rds. of S.A.A.
At each Section H.Q. 12,000 rds. of S.A.A..
" " Coy. H.Q. 48,000 " " "
" Battn. H.Q. 144,000 " " "

At reserve emplacements. :-
8,000 rds. of S.A.A. in Right Sub Section.
12,000 " " " " Centre "
20,000 " " " " LE BLANC SABLON CH. LINE.

With reserve Coy. full complement of belt boxes and 76,000 rds. of S.A.A..
With reserve sections of Right and Centre Coys. - full complement of belt boxes, and 12,000 rds. of S.A.A. per Section.

For armour piercing S.A.A. see paragraph No. 3

ST. ETIENNE GUNS. (6). Coy. Commanders in whose sections St. Etienne guns are located are responsible for the administration of their personnel and for the tactical employment of the guns.

The four guns south of CRAONNELLE will be administered and rationed by O.C. Reserve Coy..

HARRASSING (7). Alternative positions for harrassing fire will be
FIRE. constructed by all Coy. Commanders. The following points
will be the principal targets. :-

                      OUVRAGE DE LA CARRIERE.
                      Pte. 74.25.
                      "   635.315.
                      "   48.33.
                      "   37.37.
                      "   345.445.

        Coy. Commanders will report as soon as possible the number of guns they can concentrate on each target.

COMMUNICA- (8).   O.C. Signal Section will make arrangements forth-
TIONS. with to connect up Coy. H.Q. by bury to existing buried
cable route.
        Lines will be laid to Section H.Q..

MESSAGES (9). (a). In the event of any hostile action. :-
AND
REPORTS.   A report will be sent immediately by wire, or by runner if wires are cut, to Bn. H.Q. and repeated to H.Q. of Inf. Bde. concerned, stating time, nature, extent and location of such action.

        A further report will be sent as soon as possible stating action taken, rounds fired, casualties, damage to emplacements and guns, position at time message is sent - e.g. - Situation now quiet.

Runners will be sent to P.C. CALVAIRE to meet Coy. runners

        (b). Daily Reports. :-
        Reports will reach P. C. CALVAIRE at noon daily, where they will be taken over by a despatch rider from Battn. H.Q., covering the period 10.0 am to 10.0 a.m.. In the case of any event of importance occurring between that hour and noon it will be reported by wire. Company Commanders are held personally responsible for the punctual arrival of reports at P. C. CALVAIRE.

SANITATION. (10).   Fly proof latrines and urine tubs will be located near every M.G. dug-out, set well forward from the Trench.

        Reports will be rendered that they have been constructed, and that all French latrines have been filled in, by noon May 25th.

                                        A.H. Morrison Lt. for Capt., & Adj..
21st. MAY, 1918.   50th. Bn., - M.G.C..

Copies to :-
   (1). - Commanding Officer.
   (2). - O.C. Signal Section.
   (3). - Lt. & Q.M..
   (4). -)
   (5). -)
   (6). -) Conference.
   (7). -)
   (8). - 149th. Inf. Bde..
   (9). - 150th. " "
  (10). - 151st. " "
  (11). - 50th. Division - G.
  (12). - War Diary.
  (13). - " "
  (14). - File.

Appendix 3

SECRET.

Ref., Map
BERRY-AU-BAC M.D., 1/10,000.

Copy No. 13.

50th. BATTALION, MACHINE GUN CORPS.

ORDER NO. 5.

14th. MAY, 1918.

Alteration of Gun Positions.

(1). The following alterations will take place in the positions of Vickers Guns and St. Etienne Guns :-

    (a) Four Vickers Guns at present situated - (1) in Boyau TOURCOING. (2) In Trench D'Epinal. (3 & 4) In Centre TARCENAU will exchange positions with four St Etienne Guns sited E. & W. of the BUTTE d'EDMOND.

    (b) Four Vickers Guns at present situated in Trench d'AMPACH will exchange positions with four St. Etienne Guns sited at OUV-du-TOULON and OUV-du-la-HUTTE.

    (c) Completion to be reported by 6-0 a.m., May 15th., by the Code Word "CRAONNE".

Command.

(2). Company Commanders will be responsible for the administration and tactical handling of St. Etienne Guns and Teams in their respective areas, and will at once get into touch with Lieut., Ford IXth. Corps Cyclist Detachment, whose Head-quarters are in the bretelle CRAONNE la HUTTE near CRAONNE, in order to ascertain exact position of Guns.

Tasks of Guns.

(3). Generally speaking the tasks of Guns will not be altered.
In order, however, to ensure that the gap in the line W. of BOIS de L'ERMULE is adequately commanded; O/C., "C" Company will make such alteration in the emplacements of Guns situated in DARCY Trench as to enable them to direct fire on to the gap should the situation demand it.

Reconnaissance.

(4). (a) O/C., "D" Company will send his Second-in-Command and Three other Officers to report to Major BALDWIN, commanding 7th. Field Company, R.E., at Point 52.85 at 2.0 p.m., May 15th., to reconnoitre emplacements and lines of approach to the Intermediate line.

He will himself reconnoitre the line with the remainder of his Officers on May 16th., and will ensure by the night of the 18th., all Gun Commanders know their positions and routes to these positions.

    (b) O/C., "A" Company will ensure that positions for the Guns of his Section at rest are constructed in the neighbourhood of the BUTTE de L'EDMOND, and that all Officers and Gun Commanders are acquainted with these positions.

    O/C., "C" Company will similarly ensure that the positions for the Guns of his resting section are constructed in the neighbourhood of LA HUTTE, with special reference to an attack from the East and North-East.

    (c). A report will be rendered to this office by mid-day, 19th. May, with sketch maps attached showing positions selected, rendezvous for Sections, and routes to Gun Positions.

Capt., & Adj.,
for Lieut.-Colonel, Cmdg.,
50th. Battalion,
MACHINE GUN CORPS.

Copies to. :-

(1). Commanding Officer.
(2). O/C., " A " Company.
(3). "   " B "   "
(4). "   " C "   "
(5). "   " D "   "
(6). "   IXth. Corps Cyclist Detachment.
(7). "   7th. Field Company, R.E.'s..
(8). 50th. Division, " G "..
(9). 149th. Infantry Brigade.
(10). 150th.   "   "
(11). 151st.   "   "
(12). War Diary.
(13).
(14). File.

- - - - - - -

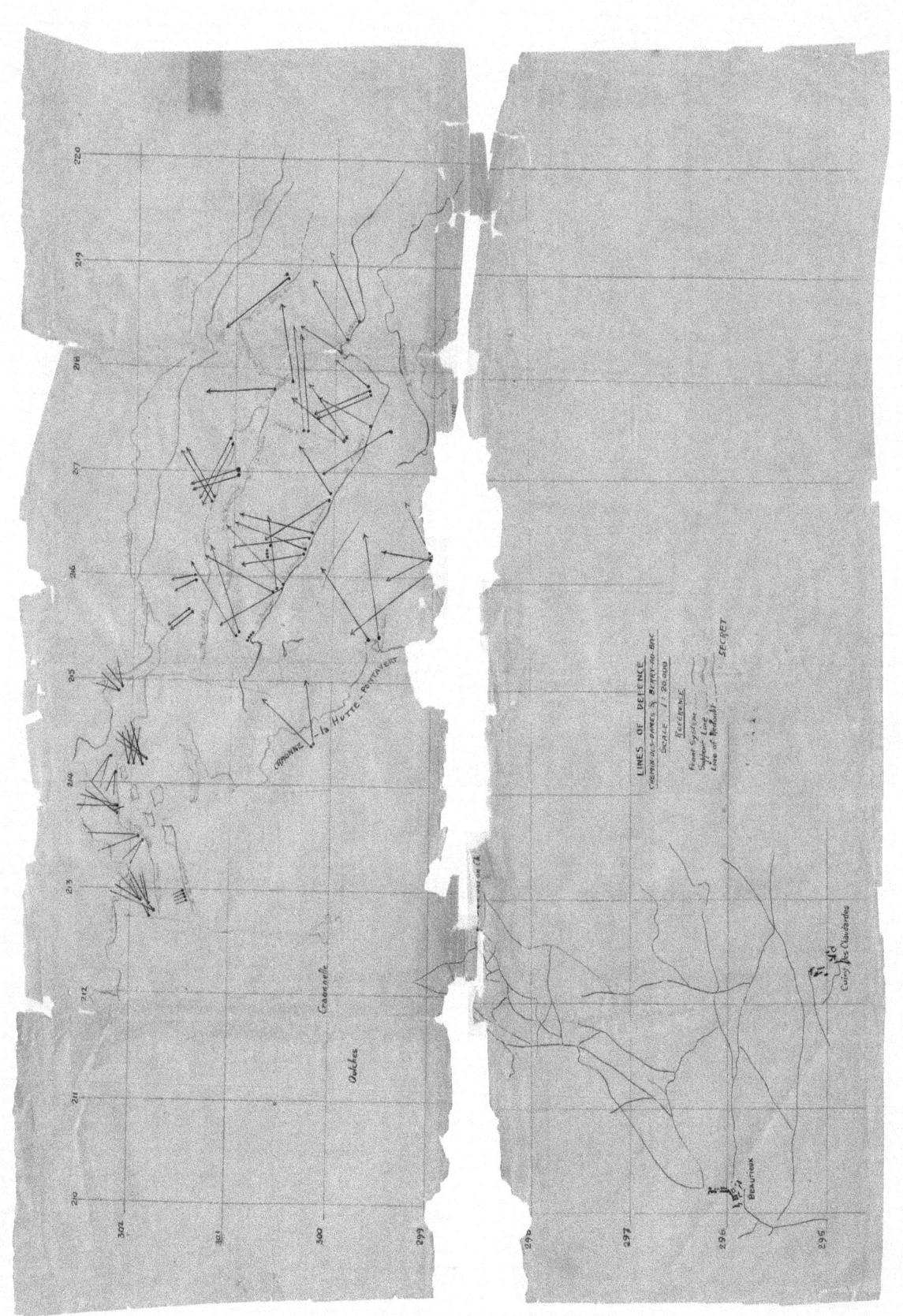

Volume III.   **Confidential.**

D.y/50

War Diary
of
50th. Batt. M.G.C.

From June 1st. 1918.
To   June 30th 1918.

WAR DIARY
or
INTELLIGENCE SUMMARY.
(Erase heading not required.)

Army Form C. 2118.

Place	Date	Hour	Summary of Events and Information	Remarks and references to Appendices
In the line	1st		Orders received at 10 AM to move CONGY and arrived at 3.30 PM	OH
	2nd	12.15 PM	Reference orders received from 50th Div. 5 officers 180 machine gunners and 3 guns, also 2 officers and 60 O.R. from the 149th Inf. Bde under the command of MAJOR T. MORRIS D.S.O. passed at 10 AM in readiness to proceed to the 149th Division. The G.O.C. 50th Div. inspected the company at 10.30 AM. At 11 AM the company proceeded to the bivouac area in huts behind.	OH
	3rd	at 2 PM	Reference 50th Division order No 212. The Battalion moved by road to Vert LA GRAVELLE, in billets being available the huts broached in groups 2 hundreds N.E. of Village. O.C. handed with G.O.C. 50th Div. and also conferred with BRIGADIER GENERAL LUCAS, M.G. Off. office G.H.Q. The C.O. visited the company in the line. At 10 AM the C.O. inspected the Battalion and trans. kit.	OH
	4th		Thirteen vickers guns sent to companies in the line having carried out under Battalion arrangements.	OH
	5th		Training carried out under Battalion arrangements. At 2.30 PM the C.O.	OH

WAR DIARY
or
INTELLIGENCE SUMMARY.

Army Form C. 2118.

Place	Date	Hour	Summary of Events and Information	Remarks and references to Appendices
Falth Rest	5th		(continued) Gave a short lecture to officers h C.O's and men on the recent fighting	OM
	6th		Training for details under Battalion arrangements. Tactical M.G. scheme carried out during the evening.	OM
	7		Training for details carried out under Battalion arrangements	OM
	8		Training for details carried out under Battalion arrangements - M.G. tactical scheme once again in the evening. C.O. lectured to the Bn. on the new German tank.	OM
	9		Battalion moved by road to the Chateau at Chipram.	OM
	10		Parades in details under Battalion arrangement. The I.O, Adjt, M.G. officer conferred with the R.O.	OM
	11		Parades in details under Br. arrangements.	OM
	12		Bathing and Musketry on the range for Bn. details	OM
	13		Bathing and musketry on the range for Bn. details	OM
	14		Tactical scheme carried out during the evening. Parades under Br. arrangements. C.O. visited the Coy in the line.	OM
	15		Bathing and Musketry in the morning. Divisional band in the evening.	OM

WAR DIARY
or
INTELLIGENCE SUMMARY.
(Erase heading not required.)

Army Form C. 2118.

Place	Date	Hour	Summary of Events and Information	Remarks and references to Appendices
	16		Played to the Bn in the afternoon	
	17		Church parades. C.O. attended conference at Divisional H.Q.	A4
	18		Bathing and gun-fitting in morning, recreational training in afternoon. Company in the	App A4
	19		Bathing and gun-fitting in morning. Company in the morning. Companies were relieved by A & G Coys of the 2nd Bn.	A4
	19		Divine service.	A4
	20		Company marched to the Bn at the Chateau at Crecy. Kit inspection by the C.O. & 2/Lt Bn.	A4
	21		Usually employed following up details, the Company from the one parade under Bn arrangements.	A4
	22		Draft of 60 O.R. arrived from M & here Coys. C.O. inspected the Draft. Parade for Bn under Bn arrangements	A4
	23		Church parade by morning.	A4
	24		Parades under Battalion arrangements. eight guns carried	A4

WAR DIARY or INTELLIGENCE SUMMARY

Place	Date	Hour	Summary of Events and Information	Remarks and references to Appendices
	24		Adv. party twelve at the range at VERDEY. Preges into battalion arrangement. Down Ga. officers	C47
	25		inspected all P.B. n.o. of the Bn.	C47
			C.O. accompanied the line Col. H.C. Sheriff to the Bn. Parade ordered. Bn. arrangements 25 officers and	C47
	26			
	27		4.50 O.R. arrived for the Bn. C.O. inspected to Duft. Parade for the Commander of the Bn. carried out under bn arrangements.	C47
	28		13 Coy (less one) on the range at VERDEY. remainder	C47
	29		of the Bn. banned into Coy arrangements 1 Coy fires on range at VERDEY, 1 Coy ar. at the (b) range at LACHY for musketry.	C47
	30		Changed hands.	C47

Volume IV

Confidential.

War Diary
of
50th. Batt. M.G.C.

From July 1st. 1918.
To July 31st. 1918.

WAR DIARY
or
INTELLIGENCE SUMMARY.
(Erase heading not required.)

Army Form C. 2118.

Place	Date	Hour	Summary of Events and Information	Remarks and references to Appendices
	1st July		Ref 50th Div operation order No 224 & Bn order no 7 Battalion moved by road to LENTHES. Weather very fine all day.	CH Appendix No (6)
	2nd		Ref 50th Div operation order No 226 & Bn order no 8 Battalion moved by road to VASSIMONT area. Two companies and HQ billeted in VASSIMONT and two companies in HAUSSIMONT. Weather very fine.	CH No (6) Appendix
	3rd		Ref 50th Div operation order No 229 & Bn order no 9. Battalion marched to TAMMASIOUS and entrained weather became fine. Battalion detrained at MARGET at 6.30 PM and arrived at FAVERNY arrived at 11 PM. Weather very fine.	CH No (C)
	4th		Parades under Bn arrangements.	CH
	5th		Parades under Bn arrangements. Colonel Chateris relieved the Bn. the CO. motored to 4th Army HQ. Nothen Freres Perspue	CH
	6th		Parades under Bn arrangements. C.O. attended conference at 4th Army by G.O.C. Reference at 4 PM, weather fine.	CH
	7th		Ref 50th Div operation order No 229 & Bn order No 10 Bn moved by road to CURAVILLE area High and three companies	CH Appendix No 2

WAR DIARY
or
INTELLIGENCE SUMMARY.
(Erase heading not required.)

Army Form C. 2118.

Place	Date	Hour	Summary of Events and Information	Remarks and references to Appendices
	7th July		were billeted at MEULLEVILLE and one company at GUEUVILLE. Parades under Coy arrangements. Weather very fine.	207
	8th		Companies reconnoitred the training area. The C.O. and 2i/c 2nd A.C. weather fine.	207
	9th		Training under Coy arrangements. Weather very fine	207
	10th		Ref B.M.G 282. The Battalion moved by road to CANDESCURE.	207
			During the afternoon C Coy carried out a belted scheme A, B & D Coys on the ranges. Weather fine, hot during morning, rain in afternoon.	A/A Sw No 3
	11th		Training under Coy arrangements. Weather fine in morning, rain in afternoon	207
	12th		Training under Coy arrangements. Divisional General inspected 2i/c the C.O. weather fine 1 shower all day)	207
	13th		Training under Coy arrangements. Weather fine, rain on & off day	207
	14th		Training under Coy arrangements. C.O inspected men little	207
			Coy commanders conference. Weather fine, stormy all day	
	15th		Training under Coy arrangements. Weather fine, showery all day	207
	16		Training under Coy arrangements. Weather fine, fine during day	207

WAR DIARY
or
INTELLIGENCE SUMMARY.
(Erase heading not required.)

Army Form C. 2118.

Place	Date	Hour	Summary of Events and Information	Remarks and references to Appendices
	17th		Training under Coy arrangements. Weather great change	Coy
	18th		Training under Coy arrangements. Weather great change	Coy
	19th		Training during morning under Coy arrangements. Night operations carried out. Weather fine	Coy
	20th		C.O. inspected mounted section. Training under Coy arrangements.	Coy
			Weather fine	Coy
	21st		C.O. lectured to all officers and N.C.O's. Col. Chetwin visited the battalion. Weather front very stormy.	Coy
	22nd		Training under Coy arrangements. Weather great change	
	23rd		Training under Coy arrangements. Weather front stormy	Coy
	24th		Training under Coy arrangements. Start of section competition.	Coy
			Pilot Cavalry a'left Albright reports in – the judging rather heat storm	
	25th		Training under Coy arrangements. 2nd day of section competition.	Coy
			Weather front fair	
	26th		Training under Coy arrangements. 3rd day of section competition. Col Chetwin assisted in the judging. Weather great fine all day	Coy

WAR DIARY
or
INTELLIGENCE SUMMARY.

Army Form C. 2118.

Place	Date	Hour	Summary of Events and Information	Remarks and references to Appendices
	27th		Training outer. Coy arrangements. 1st day of section competition.	C.U.T.
	28th		The C.O. motored to ARKVILLE and visited the camouflage works. Church parade. weather front very fine. stormy	C.U.T
	29th		Ref. III Cops operation order no 286 & Bn Order No 11. The Battalion moved by road to OISEMONT. weather present very fine all day.	out
	30th		Ref. III Corps operation order no 266 & Bn order No 11. The Battalion marched to CONDÉ. weather present very fine all day.	C.U.2 appx
	31st		Ref. III Corps operation order no. 266 & Bn order No 11. The Battalion marched FRESSELLES. weather present very fine all day.	app No 4.

50th Bn. M.G.C. ORDER No. 8.

Ref: MAP
N.W. Europe
1/250,000.

Appendix No 1(B)

Copy No. _____

MOVE
1.
The Bn. will move to VASSIMONT and HAUSSIMONT tomorrow July 2nd at 10.10 a.m. Starting point - junction of SEZANNE - FER-CHAMPNOISE and LINTHELLES - LINTHES Road.

ORDER OF MARCH.
2.
H.Qrs. "B", "C", "D", "A" Coys. Cookers will accompany Coys. - remainder of transport at rear of column (same distances as today will be observed).

DINNERS.
3.
A halt will be made for dinners at 12.30 p.m. and the Bn. will move off again at 2.0 p.m.

ADVANCE PARTIES.
4.
One Officer per Coy. will report to 2nd Lt. DOUCHE at 8.30 a.m. and will proceed direct to the billeting area.
One mounted orderly will be sent back to Eastern exits CONNANTRY to report to the Commanding Officer at 1.30 p.m. at th the location of B.H.Q. and the approximate number that can be billeted in each village.

BILLETING CERTIFICATES.
5.
Coy. Commanders will render to B.H.Q. by 8 a.m. the exact number of Officers in billets and O.R. together with names of owners.

CLAIMS.
6.
Coy. Commanders will ensure that all claims for damage are submitted before 8.30 a.m.

SANITATION.
7.
All Latrines will be carefully filled in and horse lines, billets and bivouacs are left scrupulously clean.

REPORT on MEN FALLING OUT.
8.
A report as to the number of men falling out will be rendered on arrival.

(Signed) C.V. FORSLIND,
Capt. A/Adjt.
50th Bn. M.G.C.

Issued at 8.30 p.m.

Copies to :-
1 Commanding Officer.
2 "A" Coy.
3 "B" "
4 "C" "
5 "D" "
6 T.O.
7 Q.M.
8)
9) War Diary.
10. File.

50th Bn. M.G.C. Order No. 9.   SECRET.

Reference :-   Copy No. 11.
Map France Sheet 10.
1/250,000.

MOVE   1. The Battalion will move to SOMESOUS tomorrow July 3rd,
                where it will entrain.
                Companies will move as follows :-
            1. A. and C. Coys. transport including cookers and filled
                water carts will leave HAUSSIMONT at 8.30 a.m. O.C. A. Coy.
                will detail responsible officer to report to Capt. COCHRANE,
                4th E. York. R. at the station at 8.50 a.m. This officer
                will hand one copy of entraining state for A. & C. Coys. complete
                with Transport to Capt. COCHRANE: second copy will be handed
                to Capt. F.A. FOLEY, 4th York R., detraining officer, on
                arrival at destination. This state will be prepared by O.C.
                A. Coy.
            2. A. & C. Coys. will leave HAUSSIMONT at 10.20 a.m. under
                the command of Major BROOKS. They will report to Major MORRIS,
                D.S.O., on arrival at SOMESOUS station. Both Coys. will leave
                SOMESOUS at 12.15 p.m. under command of Major MORRIS, D.S.O.
            3. The remainder of the Battalion will leave VASSIMONT at 12
                noon. Transport will move at the head of the column and will
                report to 2nd Lt. W.H. DOUCHE at SOMESOUS station. It will
                not halt at 12.50 p.m. The train will leave at 4.18 p.m.
                2nd Lt. W.H. DOUCHE will be provided with two copies of
                entraining state of B.H.Q., and B. and D. Companies.

ADVANCED
PARTY.   2. Lt. J.S. MACHIN and one N.C.O. per Company will report to
                Capt. FOLEY, 4th York R. at SOMESOUS at 5. 0 a.m. The
                Q.M. will arrange to issue five bicycles. Three days rations
                will be taken. Lt. J.S. MACHIN will obtain from Battalion
                Headquarters a copy of the Battalion Entraining State.

SUPPLIES.   3. One days train rations will be drawn at SOMESOUS.

BILLETING
CERTIFICATES. 4. O.C. A. Company will ensure that Billeting Certificates
                are completed, and that a certificate that no claims are
                outstanding is received from the Mayor of HAUSSIMONT by 9.30 a.m.
                O.C. B. & D. Coys. will render Billeting statements
                to Battalion Headquarters by the same hour.

SANITATION. 5. Coy. Commanders will ensure that all Latrines are filled
                in, and that all billets are left in a clean and sanitary
                condition.

WATER CARTS. 6. No water will be drawn from water carts after 9.30 a.m.
                at which hour carts will proceed to refill.

                                                        Capt. & Adjt.
                                                        50th Bn. M.G.C.

2nd July, 1918.

Issued at 7.30 p.m.
Copies to :-
1 to 5   C. O. and Coy. Cmdrs.
6   T. O.
7   Q. M.
8   Lt. Machin.
9   2nd Lt. Douche.
10.   2nd in Command.
11 & 12   War Diary.
13 & 14   File.

Reference:-
BOD + DIEPPE.
1/100,000.

50th Bn. M.G.C.   No. 13.

SECRET.

Copy No. _____

Appendix No. 7 N

1. **MOVE.** The Battalion will move to GUIGNVILLE tomorrow, July 7th, at 11.0 a.m. Starting point, road junction ½ Mile W. of E in EPECOURT.

2. **ORDER OF MARCH.** H.Qrs. C. D. A. B. Cookers will accompany Companies; transport will move in the rear. Officer's Mess Cart will move off at 10.30 a.m. and will report to the Commanding Officer at the Mairie, GUIGNVILLE on arrival.

3. **ROUTE.** Vaux, Oisemont, Cannaches.

4. **DINNERS.** A Halt for dinners will be made at 12.30 p.m. until 2.00 p.m.

5. **BILLETING CERTIFICATES.** Billeting Certificates will be handed in without fail to Bn. Orderly Room by 9. 0 a.m.

6. **ADVANCED PARTIES.** 2nd Lt. W.H. DOUGHE and one Officer and one N.C.O. per Company, will report to the Commanding Officer at the Mairie, GUIGNVILLE at 1.0 p.m. They will take haversack rations.

7. **SANITATION.** Company Commanders will ensure that all latrines are filled in and that all billets are left in a scrupulously clean condition.

8. **CLAIMS.** All claims for damage or loss will be presented to Bn. H.Qrs. by 9.0 a.m.

9. **TENTS.** Tents will be struck and stacked at the entrance to the Chateau by 8.0 a.m. at which hour the transport will convey them to the Area Commandant, HUPPY.

Issued at 12 midnight
6th July, 1918.

Capt. & Adjt.
50th Bn. M. G. C.

To :-
"A" Coy. "B" Coy.
"C" Coy. "D" Coy.
T.O. Q.M. & R.S.M.

M.G. 287.

Unless contrary orders are received Coys. will move independently this afternoon to GRANDCOURT. Bn. H.Qrs. will move off at 2.0 p.m. "A" Coy. will move between 2.15 and 2.30 p.m. "B" Coy. between 2.30 and 2.45 p.m. "C" Coy. between 2.45 and 3.0 p.m. "D" Coy. between 3.0 and 3.15 p.m.

Certificates as to cleanliness of billets will be forwarded to Bn. H.Qrs. by 2.0 p.m.

O.C. Coys. will arrange for the transport of their sick on limbers.

Representatives of Coys. will meet 2nd Lt. DOUCHE at the Maire at GRANDCOURT at 10.15 a.m.

Billeting Certificates will be forwarded to Bn. H.Qrs. immediately.

Capt. & Adjt.
50th Bn. M.G.Corps.

9th July, 1918.

It is to be understood that the personnel of Coys. will move on the completion of training direct to GRANDCOURT. The courses mentioned in Bn. Order No. 5 dated 8-7-18 will commence notwithstanding the move.

Reference :-
1/10,000 Maps.
Nos. 16, 14 & 11.

50th Bn. M.G.C. ORDER No. 11.

SECRET.

Copy No. 71

Move 1. The Bn. will commence to move to the III Corps area, on 29th July, in accordance with attached march table.

PACKS 2. All Packs and Blankets will be stacked at Coy. Q.M. Stores at 6.30 a.m. ready to be loaded on lorries which will call for them.

The rear half limbers for which there are no corresponding fore portions will be at Q.M. Stores at 9.0 p.m. tonight, 28.7.18 dismantled and ready for placing on lorries.

CLAIMS & CERTIFICATES 3. Billeting Certificates will be forwarded to Bn.Qr.Mr. by 8.0 a.m.

Certificates re cleanliness of billets will be handed in at Bn. Orderly Room by 9.0 a.m. The greatest care will be exercised to ensure that billets and the surrounding areas are left scrupulously clean.

Claims for damage will be forwarded to Bn. Orderly Room by 8.0 a.m.

BILLETING PARTIES 4. Billeting parties of 1 Officer and 1 N.C.O. per Coy, and the R.Q.M.S., will report to 2nd Lt. W.H.DOUCHE at Bn.Qr.Mr. Stores at 7.45 a.m. and will proceed to OISEMONT on lorries. On arrival the party will report to the Purchase Board Officer for allotment of billets.

Billeting parties will meet the Coys. at a point quarter mile outside western outskirts of OISEMONT.

Capt. & Adjt.
50th Bn. M.G.Corps.

Issued at   p.m. 28.7.18.
Copies to :-
1.   C.O.
2 - 5   Coys.
6.   Asst. Adjt.
7.   Q.M.
8.   2nd Lt. W.H.Douche.
9.   Area Commandant.
10. M.O.
11.& 12 War Diary.
13. File.

Confidential

Vol 6

War Diary
of
50th Bn. M.G.C.

Volume 4.

From August 1st 1918
To August 31st 1918.

WAR DIARY
or
INTELLIGENCE SUMMARY

Army Form C. 2118.

Place	Date	Hour	Summary of Events and Information	Remarks and references to Appendices
At Rest	1st Aug		Ref 50th Bn M.G.C. operation order No 12. 4th Battalion moved from FLESSELLES to QUERRIEU area. Bn Hqrs, A & D Coys billeted in QUERRIEU, Bn Hqrs QUERRIEU CHATEAU, B & C Coys bivouac. Heavy rain fell all day.	CIV
				Appendix No 1
	2nd		Ref 50th Bn M.G.C. order No 13. B & C Coys relieved M.G. Coys of the 2nd LIFE GUARDS and came under orders of the 47th & 56th Divs respectively.	CIV
			Reconnaissance & administration. D Coy attached to 16th Div and went into A Coys rendezvous at QUERRIEU in Corps reserve. Major Leehan commanded M.G. officers visited the Bn. Weather very unsettled. Heavy rain in the evening.	Appendix No 2
	3		The C.O went on leave to U.K. Major J.M. Moore Lt.Col Commanded of the Bn. B C & D Coys in reserve to their respective divisions. Weather dull. Little rain	CIV
	4		Div Hqrs at QUERRIEU Chateau and were billets in QUERRIEU village. Cols M.G. officers visits the battalion. Artillery very active all along Corps front. Weather unsettled	CIV
	5		Gen LUCAS & Col CHARTERIS visited the Battalion. Our bivouac withstood a heavy downpour, and saw A Coy training. Sky clearing. Enemy withdrew on 16th Div front. Artillery very active. Weather warm and dry.	CIV
	6		Large hostile raid on 18th Div front, in which a number of prisoners were taken. Our Artillery very active. Weather fine	CIV

Army Form C. 2118.

WAR DIARY
or
INTELLIGENCE SUMMARY.
(Erase heading not required.)

Instructions regarding War Diaries and Intelligence Summaries are contained in F. S. Regs., Part II. and the Staff Manual respectively. Title pages will be prepared in manuscript.

Place	Date	Hour	Summary of Events and Information	Remarks and references to Appendices
In the field	7th		Enemy very active all day, several attacks of his artillery. Hostile aero were shelled continuously. Weather very fine. Casualties 12 O.R. wounded	Cas
	7th		South Army attack at dawn. 50th Bn M.G.C. relies in in concelled	Cas
	8th			Appendix 3
	9th		Casualties D Coy 1 O.R. killed, 1 O.R. wounded, weather very fine all day. Ref 50th Bn M.G.C. order no 15, B: Hqts & C. Coy moved to BONNAY via LAHOUSSOYE. B. Coy moved into 58th Div area and came under command of 58 Div. A Coy moved to FRAMVILLERS & came under orders of 12th Div. Casualties nil. Weather very fine.	Appendix 4
	10th		Ref 50th Bn M.G.C. order No 16. The battalion concentrated at GOCKNIED. Major J.H. GARDINER went on leave to U.K. Capt C.H.M. TOY took command of C. Coy. weather very fine.	OH. eng Appendix No 5
	11th		Training carried out under B. arrangements. The O.C. reconnoitred part of the line with the Corps M.G. officer. Weather very fine.	Cas
	12th		Training carried out under B: arrangements. Very fine.	
	13		Corps reconnoitered reserve line in Corps area. Two infantry officers have reported for duty a subaltern officers. Ref 50th Bn G.C order no 17	

WAR DIARY
or
INTELLIGENCE SUMMARY.

(Erase heading not required.)

Army Form C. 2118.

Place	Date	Hour	Summary of Events and Information	Remarks and references to Appendices
In the field	13		The Bn. less A Coy moved to BONNAY in Corps reserve. A Coy moved into the line South of VILLE SOUS CORBIE. Weather very fine	Appendix 6 OO4
	14		Ref. 50th Bde M.G.C. order No 18. The Bn less A Coy moved to QUERRIEU and came under orders of the 47th Div. Coy reassembled reserve line in Corps Area. A Coy 16 Guns in old British line E. of MORLANCOURT.	Appendix No 7
	15		One Coy put under two hours notice. Two Coys under four hours. Four guns of A Coy moved into new position in K.13.A. Very fine. Enemy artillery very active during night.	
	16		No enemy aeroplanes observed, our planes very active especially between H.P.S and dusk. Two companies under two hours notice one Coy under two hours notice. Weather during morning fine in afternoon	OO4
	17		Enemy Artillery less active than heavy. Our Artillery very active during night. Increase of aerial activity. One Coy under two hours notice two Coys under four hours notice. Weather very fine.	OO4
	18		Orders issued to relief of A Coy by a Coy of the 18th Div. front Bn. Artillery less active than of heavy bombardment on enemy lines from	Appendix 8

WAR DIARY
or
INTELLIGENCE SUMMARY.
(Erase heading not required.)

Army Form C. 2118.

Place	Date	Hour	Summary of Events and Information	Remarks and references to Appendices
In the field	19th		8 AM – 4.30 AM. Weather very fine. Relief of A Coy by C Coy cancelled. Ref. 60th Bn. M.G.C. order No. 20. The Bn. less A & D Coys moved to WARLOY and came under the 18th Div. A & D Coy moved to BEAUCOURT and came under orders of the 12th Div. Weather very fine.	Appendix No 9 OUR
	20th		B & C Coys came under command of 18 Bn. M.G.C., positions to give covering fire to 16th Div occupied. Coys moved up to line and commenced making shell hole emplacements at midnight. Enemy artillery very active all day & night. On artillery very quiet. Capt. J.W. Cox, replaced from M.G. Base and took command of D Coy. Weather very fine.	A14.
	21st		The C.O. returned from leave. Intermittent shelling all day. On artillery bombardt. About 10th gas during the night. Weather very fine.	OUT
	22nd		Own infantry attacked at dawn. All objectives gained. C Coy fired 71000 rounds, many targets engaged. One Section of A Coy came under barrage fire, casualties 1 OR wounded. Weather very fine. D Coy engages two enemy M.G's, one was put out of action the other only fires on relief.	CH4

WAR DIARY
or
INTELLIGENCE SUMMARY.
(Erase heading not required.)

Army Form C. 2118.

Instructions regarding War Diaries and Intelligence Summaries are contained in F.S. Regs., Part II. and the Staff Manual respectively. Title pages will be prepared in manuscript.

Place	Date	Hour	Summary of Events and Information	Remarks and references to Appendices
			and Artillery fire. 18th Divn attacked at Dawn, capturing TRONES Wood, also DELVILLE WOOD. But a counter attack drove them back to just W of LONGUEVAL. B Coy recovered a line running thence BAZENTIN LE GRAND but later in took up a line running through MONTAUBAN. A Coy took up a defensive line on the ridge S.W. of MAURICE. Casualties - 2 OR wounded. Weather stormy during night, fine all day.	MY
	28th		DELVILLE & BERNAFAY WOOD captured, during early hours of morning a battalion of Prussian Guard attacked TRONES WOOD but were completely repulsed owing to Heavy M.G. fire. Casualties nil. Weather fine.	114
	29th		Bn H.Q. moved from WARLOY to S.W. Corner of BERNAFAY WOOD. Infantry Captured LEUZE WOOD. B & C Coys in reserve to 18th Divn. A & D in reserve to 12th Div. Casualties nil. Weather fine.	114
	30		A & D Coys moved forward. Infantry Captured COMBLES. Casualties nil. Weather fine.	C04
	31		Infantry advanced to W of MORVAL & RANCOURT. A Coy assisted in barrage by Barrage fire. 3 officers & 23 O.R. reported for duty from M.G. Base. Strong hostile counter attack on 47 Divn repulsed. A & D companies both played stirring role. 8 OR killed. Weather fine. 60 R wounded.	C04

Date.	Starting Point.	Orders of March.	Time.	From.	To.	Route.	Remarks.
July 29th.	Road junction immediately North of first P in PIERREPONT.	Bn. H.Qrs. B Coy. with Cooker. C Coy. " D " " A " " Remaining transport.	10.15 a.m.	GRANDCOURT.	OISEMONT.	Rieux Rambures.	Lorries and supply waggons leave the Bn. Q.M.Store at 8.0 a.m. C Coy. will supply an escort of 1 section. Dinners. A halt for 1½ hours will be made for dinners when the Bn. reaches the cross roads North of the B of BOIS de la GAVENTIE.
30th.	Windmill one mile East of OISEMONT.	Bn. H.Qrs. C Coy. with Cooker. D " " A " " B " " Remaining transport.	10.15 a.m.	OISEMONT.	CONDE.	AIRAINES LONGPRE.	Dinners. A halt of 1½ hours will be made when the Bn. reaches the cross roads South of U in DREUIL.
31st.	Bridge between CONDE and ETOILE.	Bn.H.Qrs. D Coy.with Cooker. A Coy. " B " " C " " Remaining transport.	10.15 a.m.	CONDE.	FLESSELLES.	FLIXECOURT VIGNECOURT.	Dinners. A halt of 1½ hours will be made when the Bn. reaches the Road junction N. of D of FORET de VERGOURT.

Reference :-
1/10,000 Maps
Sheets 11 & 27.

H.Q.G.
80th Bn./Order No. 12.

SECRET.

Appendix No. 1

Copy No. 12

MOVE 1. The Bn. will march tomorrow as follows, and in this order of march :-
Bn. H.Q. "A" & "B" Coys., at 10.15 a.m. from PIRCHLIEU to QUERRIEU, via BEHENCOURT, COISY, ALLONVILLE.
Starting point PIRCHLIEU STATION.
at 10.15 a.m.
"D" & "C" Coys., from PIRCHLIEU to CORBAY, via MOLLIENS, BEAUCOURT.
Starting point Road junction 1½ miles east of PIRCHLIEU.

COMMAND 2. As from the commencement of the march "D" & "C" Coys. will be under the command of Major F.H.PASTEUR.

BILLETING 3. Billeting parties of 1 Officer and 1 N.C.O. from "A" & "B" Coys and the R.Q.M.S., will meet 2nd Lt. W.H.DOUCHE at the Bn.Q.M. at 7.45 am. Stores and proceed on lorries. On arrival at QUERRIEU they will report to 18th Division "Q" for allotment of billets.
Billeting parties of 1 Officer and 1 N.C.O. from each of "D" & "C" Coys. will report to the Bn. Q.M. at 7.45 a.m. and proceed on lorry. On arrival at CORBAY they will report to 47th Division "Q" for allotment of billets.

AMMUNITION 4. The Bn.Q.M. will send S.A.A. as follows to CORBAY by the lorry conveying the billeting party. It will be dumped at the billets of those Coys.
For "D" Coy. 52,000 rounds.
For "C" Coy. 37,500

ESCORTS 5. O.C. "D" & "C" Coys. will detail 1 N.C.O. to accompany the billeting parties for the purpose of guarding the ammunition.

DINNERS 6. The Q.M. will arrange for the cooking of the dinners of Bn. H.Q. as follows :-
½ Bn. H.Q. Dinners to be cooked by "A" Coy.
½ " " " " " " " "B" Coy.
~~Major Pasteur will arrange for the cooking of "C" Coy. dinners by "C" Coy.~~ Pasteur   B

SUPPLIES 7. Rations for consumption on 2-8-18 will be drawn by Bn.Q.M. for the whole Battalion tomorrow 1-8-18 from 3rd C.F.M.S.
The Bn. Q.M. will arrange to send the rations for "D" & "C" Coys to CORBAY during tomorrow afternoon.
Rations for consumption on 3-8-18 and subsequently will be drawn as follows commencing on 3-8-18 :-
Bn.H.Qrs. & "A" & "B" Coys. from 18th Div.
"D" & "C" Coys. from 47th Div.

ADVANCE GUARDS 8. O.C. "A" Coy. will detail one section as advanced guard to the Bn. less two Coys. Distance between Advanced guard and main body 500 yards. O.C. "A" Coy. will appoint the advanced guard commander
Major F.H.PASTEUR will detail an advanced guard of one section for "D" & "C" Coys.

a Dering
Capt. & Adjt.
80th Bn. M.G.Corps.

31st July 1918.
Issued at 9.30 p.m.
Copies to :-
1 C.O.
2 - 5 Coys.
6 Asst. Adjt.
7 Q.M.
8 2nd Lt. W.H.Douche.
9 Area Commandant.
10 M.O.
11 & 12 War Diary.
13 File.

Appendix No 2

50th Bn. M.G.C. ORDER No. 13.

SECRET.
Copy No. 4.

RELIEFS　1.　"B" & "C" Coys. will relieve two Coys. of 2nd LIFE GUARDS on the night of the 2nd/3rd August, under arrangements to be made direct with C.O. 2nd Life Guards and will come under the orders of the 47th and 58th Div. respectively for command and administration.

2.　"D" Coy. will enter the line in the 18th Divisions sector on the night of the 2nd August. O.C. "D" Coy. and representatives of sections will be at BN. H.Q. at 1.30 p.m. tomorrow, 2nd inst., mounted, and will proceed to meet the O.C. 18th Bn. M.G.C. at 2.30 p.m. at a point to be notified later.

3.　The powers of a Commanding Officer are delegated to Major F.M. PASTEUR and Major J.H. GARDNER in accordance with para. 457 K.Regs.

4. O.C.Coys. will report completion of relief to these H.Qrs.

a Devin
Capt. & Adjt.,
50th Bn. M.G.Corps.

Issued at 9.30 p.m.
1st August, 1918.
Copies to :-
1　C.O.
2 - 5 Coys.
6　Q.M.
7 & 8 War Diary.
9　File.
10. 2nd Bn. (Life Guards) Guards M.G.Regt.
11. 47th Div.
12. 58th Div.
13. 18th Bn. M.G.C.

Ref: Sheet
SENLIS
1/20,000.

Appendix No. 3

50th Bn. M.G.C. Order No. 14.

SECRET.
Copy No. 8

1. On the night of the 9th/10th Aug., "A" Coy. will relieve "D" Coy. in the line.

2. O.C. "D" Coy. will send a guide to meet the representatives of "A" Coy. at "D" Coy. transport lines in FRANVILLERS, at 11.0 a.m. The representatives of "A" Coy. will then proceed to "D" coy. H.Q. and arrange details of relief.

3. Trench stores and documents, maps, etc., relating to the sector will be handed over. Receipts will be obtained and forwarded to Bn. H.Q. on morning after the relief.

4. O.C. "A" Coy. will return the following maps to BN.H.Q. before leaving QUERRIEU :-
   - 2   1/100,000   LENS.
   - 2   do.   AMIENS.
   - 8   1/20,000   Sheet 62d N.E.
   - 8   do.   "   62d N.W.
   - 8   do.   "   57d S.E.
   - 8   do.   "   57d S.W.

5. On completion of relief "A" Coy. will come under the command of O.C. 18th Bn. M.G.C., "D" Coy. will come under the command of O.C. 50th Bn. M.G.C.

6. On completion of relief "D" Coy. will march to QUERRIEU and occupy the billets vacated by "A" Coy. "D" Coy. will send a billeting party in advance to BN.H.Q.

7. Completion of relief will be reported to Bn. H.Q. by wire using code word "SIGH".

8. ACKNOWLEDGE.

Capt. & Adjt.
50th Bn. M.G.Corps.

Issued at 7.30 p.m.
8th August, 1918.

Copies to :-
1   C.O.
2   "A" Coy.
3   "D" Coy.
4   Q.M.
5   M.O.
6   18th Bn. M.G.C.
7 & 8 War Diary.
9   File.

Ref: Maps.
1/20,000
Sheet 62d N.E.
" 62d N.W.

50th Bn. M.G.C. ORDER No. 15.

SECRET.

Copy No. 9

Appendix No 4

1. The Bn. H.Q. and "C" Company will move to BONNAY via LAHOUSSOYE. "C" Company will move independently at 6.30 p.m. tonight.

2. "B" Coy. will move to K.26.c.2.0. on receipt of these orders. On arrival they will come under orders of the 58th Division. O.C. "B" Coy. will report en route for orders at H.Q. 58th Div. at J.19.c.8.5.

3. "A" Coy. will move to FRANVILLERS on receipt of these orders where it will come under the orders of the 12th Division.

4. The relief of "D" Coy. by "A" Coy. tonight is cancelled.

5. "A" & "B" Coys. will report departure to this Office.

6. Subsequent reports to BONNAY.

A Dening
Capt. & Adjt.
50th Bn. M.G.Corps.

9th August, 1918.

Issued at   p.m.

Copies to :-
1   C.O.
2 - 5 Coys.
6   Q.M.
7   M.O.
8 & 9 War Diary.
10   File.
11   Area Commandant.
12   58th Div.
13   12th Div.

Ref. Sheet   Appendix No 5.   SECRET.
10 & 17   50th Bn. M.G.C. Order No 16.
1/100,000.   Copy No. 8.

1. The Bn. will concentrate tonight at QUERRIEU.

2. The Bn. will move on the night of the 11th/12th from QUERRIEU to left Divisional Area.

3. (a) The Bn. less three Coys. will move ~~via COMBIE~~ tonight from BONNAY to QUERRIEU, via COMBIE.
Starting point - Bn.H.Q. in BONNAY.
Starting time - Bn.H.Q. - 9.0 p.m.
                C.Coy. - 9.15 p.m.
"C" Coy. will move independently of Bn.H.Qrs. Distances will be maintained in accordance with A.R.O. 2037.

(b) "D" Coy. will withdraw the guns at present in the 18th Divisional sector in consultation with O.C. 18th Bn. M.G.C. and march to QUERRIEU tonight.

(c) "A" & "B" Coys. will move to QUERRIEU on orders of the 12th and 58th Divs. respectively.

4. Billeting parties representing each Coy. have been sent to QUERRIEU. "A", "B" & "D" Coys., will send a representative to Bn. H.Q., in QUERRIEU to meet their billeting party.

5. Rations will be drawn tomorrow morning in QUERRIEU.

                                                    A. Devine
                                                    Capt. & Adjt.
10th August, 1918.   50th Bn. M.G.Corps.

Issued at   p.m.

Copies to :-

1   C.O.
2 - 5 Coys.
6   Q.M.
7 & 8 War Diary.
9   File.
10. 18th Bn. M.G.C.

Ref: 1/100,000
Map, Sh. 17. 50th Bn. M.G.C. ORDER No. 17.

Appendix No 6

SECRET.
Copy No. 9

1. The Bn. less one Coy. will move this evening to BONNAY and will remain there in Corps Reserve. "A" Coy. will enter the line south of VILLE-sous-CORBIE.

2(a) The Bn. less one Coy. will move via LAHOUSSOYE. Coys. will move independently. Distances will be maintained in accordance with A.R.O. 2087.
   Starting point — Cross Roads N. of P in PONT NOYELLES.
   Hour of passing Starting Point. Bn. H.Q.   5.45 p.m.
                                    "B" Coy.   6. 0 p.m.
                                    "C" Coy.   6.15 p.m.
                                    "D" Coy.   6.30 p.m.

(b) "A" Coy. will move out independently at 6.0 p.m. and take up positions already reconnoitred by Section officers.

3. Lt. A.H.MORRISON will proceed to BONNAY to obtain accommodation. Billeting parties of one section complete less transport will be sent on in advance and meet Lt. A.H.MORRISON in BONNAY at 4.0 p.m.

4. Rations will be drawn at Q.M.Stores at QUERRIEU at 3.0 p.m. today.

5. Billeting Certificates and certificates as to cleanliness of billets will be forwarded to Bn. Orderly Room by 4 p.m.

6. Battle surplus of "B", "C" & "D" Coys. will move with their Coys. rejoining Bn.H.Q. at BONNAY.
   Battle surplus of "A" Coy. will move with Bn.H.Q.

7. ACKNOWLEDGE.

A Devine
Capt. & Adjt.
50th Bn. M.G.Corps.

13th August, 1918.
Issued at   p.m.

Copies to :-

1   C.O.
2   "A" Coy.
3   "B" "
4   "C" "
5   "D" "
6   Q.M.
7   Area Commandant.
8 & 9   War Diary.
10.   File.

Ref: Map
1/100,000
Sheet 17.

50th Bn. M.G.C. ORDER No. 18.

SECRET.
Copy No. 8

Appendix No 7

1. The Bn. less one Coy. will move this evening from BONMAY to QUERRIEU via LA HOUSSOYE and will remain there in Corps Reserve.

2. Coys. will move independently. Distances will be maintained in accordance with A.R.O.2037.
   Starting point - forked roads 1/3 mile North of BONMAY.
   Time of passing starting point - Bn. H. Q.   5.15 p.m.
                                    "C" Coy.   5.30 p.m.
                                    "D" Coy.   5.45 p.m.
                                    "B" Coy.   6. 0 p.m.

3. 2nd Lt. G.L. PEARSON will proceed on receipt of this order to QUERRIEU and report to Area Commandant for billeting accomodation. As far as possible Coys. and H.Q. will occupy the same billets as on 13.8.18.
   Coys. will send billeting parties in advance to meet 2nd Lt. G.L. PEARSON at the last H.Q. in QUERRIEU at 4.0 p.m.

4. Rations will be drawn by "A" Coy. at QUERRIEU at 4.0 p.m. and by the remaining Coys. on arrival at QUERRIEU.

5. Battle surplus of "B", "C" & "D" Coys. will move with their Coys. rejoining Bn.H.Q. at QUERRIEU.
   Battle surplus of "A" Coy. will move with Bn.H.Q.

6. Telephone communication between Bn. H.Q. and "A" Coy. will be maintained through QUERRIEU Exchange - III Corps - 47th Div. - 140th Bde.

7. ACKNOWLEDGE.

Issued at 2.5 p.m.
14th August, 1918.

Capt. & Adjt.
50th Bn. M.G.Corps.

Copies to :-

1   C.O.
2   "A" Coy.
3   "B" "
4   "C" "
5   "D" "
6   Q.M.
7 & 8   War Diary.
9   File.

Ref; Map.
1/20,000
Sheet 62d N.E.

50th Bn. M.G.C. ORDER No. 19.

SECRET.
Copy No. 7.

Appendix No. 8

1. "C" Coy. will relieve "A" Coy. in the old British Defences West of MORLANCOURT on the night of ~~19th/20th~~ 20th/21st August.

2. The following positions will be taken over :-

   A1 Batt. 2 guns.   K.13.d.50.60.
   A2 Batt.   do.   K.7.b.15.20
   A3 Batt.   do.   K.1.b.23.32
   A4 Batt.   do.   K.2.a.20.55.
   B1 Batt.   do.   K.13.c.00.80
   B2 Batt.   do.   J.16.b.92.83.
   B3 Batt.   do.   J.12.c.75.57.
   B4 Batt.   do.   J.6.c.60.35.

3. All Trench stores, documents, etc., will be handed over on relief and receipts obtained.

4. O.C. "C" Coy. and section officers will proceed to "A" Coy. advanced H.Q. (J.11.c.7.0) at 11 a.m. ~~19~~.8.18 20.8.18 and reconnoitre the positions.

5. All further details of relief will be arranged between Coys.

6. Completion of relief to be reported to Bn. H.Q. by wire using the code word "SAMUEL"

7. On completion of relief "A" Coy. will march back to QUERRIEU and occupy billets vacated by "C" Coy. ("A" Coy. will send a billeting party in advance.)

8. ACKNOWLEDGE.

Issued at 8.30. p.m.
18th August, 1918.

Capt. & Adjt.
50th Bn. M.G.Corps.

Copies to :-

1   C.O.
2   "A" Coy.
3   "C" Coy.
4   Q.M.
5   C.M.G.O. III Corps.
6   47th Bn. M.G.C.
7 & 8 War Diary.
9   File.

Ref: Map.
1/100,000
Sheet 27.

Appendix No 9

50th Bn. M.G.C. ORDER No. 20.

SECRET.
Copy No.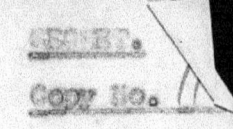

1. 50th Bn. M.G.C. Order No. 19 is cancelled.

2. The Bn. less two Coys. will move to COMBAY this evening and come under the command of 20th Division.

3. "A" & "B" Coy. will come under the command of 12th Div. O's.C. "A" & "B" Coys. will report to H.Q., 12th Div. at BEAUCOURT forthwith for orders.

4. Bn. H.Q., "D" & "C" Coys. will move independently as follows :-

Starting Point.	Hour of starting.	Route.
Bn. H.Q. Road Junction N. of last U in GUEMAPPE.	5.15 p.m.	FRESNECOURT. MONTIGNY. BEAUCOURT.
"C" Coy. do.	5.30 p.m.	do.
"D" Coy. Cross roads N. of P in FORT HOUDAINS.	5.45 p.m.	FRESNECOURT. BEAUCOURT.

   Distances will be maintained in accordance with A.R.O. 607.

5. Capt. J.A. MIDDLETON will proceed to COMBAY forthwith and report to 20th Div. H.Q. for accommodation for Bn. H.Q. and two Coys.
   "D" & "C" Coys. and Bn. H.Q., will send billeting party in advance to COMBAY on receipt of these orders to meet Capt. Middleton at COMBAY Church.

6. Billeting Certificates and certificates of cleanliness of billets will be forwarded to Bn. O.R. by 8.0 p.m.

7. Battle surplus of "A" & "B" Coys. and Recoystaining Class will move with Bn. H.Q. Battle surplus of "D" & "C" Coys. will move with their Coys.

8. Coys. on detachment will forward duplicate returns and reports to Bn. H.Q. and to the Div. by whom they are administered. The Bn. daily return will continue to be rendered.

9. ACKNOWLEDGE.

Issued at 4.0 p.m.
10th August, 1918.

A Dering
Capt. & Adjt.,
50th Bn. M.G.Corps.

Copies to :-

1	C.O.
2	"A" Coy.
3	"B" "
4	"C" "
5	"D" "
6	Q.M.
7	C.M.G.O., III Corps.
8	12th Div.
9	20th Div.
10 & 11	War Diary.
12	File.
13	Area Commandant.

Confidential

Volume VI

War Diary
of
50th. Bn. M.G.C.

From Sept 1st. 1918
To Sept 30th. 1918

WAR DIARY
or
INTELLIGENCE SUMMARY

Army Form C. 2118.

Place	Date	Hour	Summary of Events and Information	Remarks and references to Appendices
	Sept.1.		A + D coys assisted the 47th Division in their successful attack on RANCOURT. A coy harassing ALF CUT + ACILE AV. in C.B.d. D Coy harassed the northern outskirts of RANCOURT + main BOUCHAVESHES RANCOURT RD. C coy carried out harassing fire in area T17a + T23b+d. B coy were in 18th Divisional reserve at TRONIES WOOD. 18th Division captured SAILLY SAILLISEL, FREGICOURT, and PRIEZ FARM. Casualties 5. O.R. killed + 5 O.R. wounded. Weather fine.	
	2		The 47th Division in conjunction with the 18th Division successfully attacked ST PIERRE VAAST WOOD. A + D coys assisted by carrying out harassing fire. B coy moved to COMBLES. C coy remained at that disposition. Casualties 2 O.R. killed, + 4 O.R. wounded. Weather fine.	
	3		A coy remained in last disposition. D coy held line of GERMAIN TRENCH in C.10.d. B + C coys located at COMBLES. Casualties 1 O.R. wounded. Ckt. Weather showery	

WAR DIARY or INTELLIGENCE SUMMARY

Army Form C. 2118.

Place	Date	Hour	Summary of Events and Information	Remarks and references to Appendices
	4		A coy moved forward to BOUCHAVESNES QUARRY. B, C & D coys remaining in Inf. dispositions. 100th Batt. M.M.G. arrived at TRONES WOOD. III Corps Operation Order 313+4 received. 18th Division Operation Order. 224 received. Weather fine. Casualties 1 O.R. wounded.	
	5		B & C coys relieved by 2 coys of 100th Batt M.M.G. Headquarters A & D coys relieved during night of 5/6 th by the 190th Batt. B & C coys marched to RIBEMONT-SUR-ANCRE where they billeted. Weather very fine.	
	6		A & D coys proceeded by march route to RIBEMONT-SUR-ANCRE. A coy bivouaced for the night at MEAULTE. hut.gis.	
	7		Batt. H.Q. left BERNAFAY WOOD for RIBEMONT. New Bn H.Q. rejoined Batt at RIBEMONT. better fine	

WAR DIARY
INTELLIGENCE SUMMARY

(Erase heading not required.)

Army Form C. 2118.

Place	Date	Hour	Summary of Events and Information	Remarks and references to Appendices
	Sept 8		Left Bn Order No 22. Bn entrained at MERICOURT L'ABBE and proceeded to ARQUES LA BATAILLE to reorganise. Following details arranged for	Appendix 1.
	9		Corps Memo of the front of his command. G.O.C. visited the C.O. See the Coy lines.	
	10		Bn bathed, all clothing disinfected. Musketry instruction during the morning. The whole of the Bn by the M.O. gentleman.	
	11		C.O. inspected Bn by coys in their lines, comments under coy arrangements. 10 rather fine.	
	12		Divisional Tactical Scheme. Sgt B. [?] were killed [?] to indemnify. Smith [?] 5 officers were killed. Attended. 50 th finals. 85 O.R. wounded from Bn before. Wounded to the No 238 General Bus returned by Bn Concert Party. C.O. attended.	Appendix 2.
	13		C.O. inspected draft which arrived yesterday. Bn had Coy training under Coy arrangements. G.O.C. dined with C.O. Weather fine.	
	14		G.O.C. inspected the Bn + turnout in the S.B.R's of A + B coys inspected + tested in the Ant. K.C.O. went to Divisional for Cavalry Manoeuvres. 50 Strong proceeded to No 239 General from here No 239 General. Weather very fine.	

WAR DIARY
or
INTELLIGENCE SUMMARY

Army Form C. 2118.

Place	Date	Hour	Summary of Events and Information	Remarks and references to Appendices
	15th		Church Parade. Fr. a limited number of the Bn. M.O. believed Bn in town hospital. Authorised movements. Weather very fine.	
	16		Def. Bn. Order No 23. Bn entrained at ROUXMESNIL for DOULLENS. Weather fine.	Appendix 1
	17		Bn. Hdqrs & A + D Coys. lected at COULLEMONT. B + C Coys at HUMBERCOURT. Weather. Heavy showers during early morning. C.O. signed at trench & early morn.	
	18		Training under company arrangements. C.O. attended conference at Brig. H.Q. Seventy five (75) division football competition. 56th Bath. M.G.C. & SCOTTISH HORSE 3 goals to nil. Weather very fine.	
	19		C.O. inspected the Bn. by Coys at COULLEMONT 2nd in Command inspected transport limbs &c during the afternoon. Weather. Very fine.	

CAB

WAR DIARY
or
INTELLIGENCE SUMMARY

Army Form C. 2118

Place	Date	Hour	Summary of Events and Information	Remarks and references to Appendices
	20th		Training under Coy arrangements. C.O. & 3 Coy Commanders conferred with Brigade Commander. 3 Officers returned to duty from M.G. School. Weather Showery.	MH
	21		C.O. attended a conference at the HOTEL DE VILLE at DOULLENS. Coy Commanders lectured & demonstrated to the senior officers of the three Brigades. 2 O.O.R. reported for duty from the 63rd Division. Very wet all day.	MH
	22		Church Parade. Officers & N.C.O's attended lecture on co-operation of TANKS & Infantry. Rained most of day.	MH
	23		C.O. inspected the Battle Surplus of the Bn. being carried out under Coy arrangements. Weather Showery.	MH
	24		Training under Coy arrangement, including a demonstration of entering a town by means of MUD PIE model. Weather Showery.	MH
	25		Training under Coy arrangements. Weather fine. C.O. watched Bayonet fighting by Coys. Transport my first experience on lap. CMM	MH

WAR DIARY
or
INTELLIGENCE SUMMARY

(Erase heading not required.)

Army Form C. 2118.

Instructions regarding War Diaries and Intelligence Summaries are contained in F. S. Regs., Part II. and the Staff Manual respectively. Title Pages will be prepared in manuscript.

Place	Date	Hour	Summary of Events and Information	Remarks and references to Appendices
	26		Bn entrained for CONTAY SUB AREA. H.Q. B+C Coys being located at ST. GRATIEN. A+D Coys at FRECHENCOURT. Was the fine.	
	27		Training and coy arrangements. Bn transferred to MEAULTE SUB AREA. Ref. Bi Order No. 24 x Weather fine.	Appendix 4 & 3
	28		G.O.C. & staff & G.O.C. Bn left ST GRATIEN & proceeded to the embussing point, where they left for the MOISLAINS area. Battalion buses proceeded to POULAINVILLE. Weather very showery. Ref B Order No. 25	Appendix 5
	29		Training and coy arrangements. Weather showery.	
	30		Training and coy arrangements. Weather fine.	

Cranmer

Ref: 50th Bn. M.G.C. ORDER No. 22.   SECRET.
1/40,000 Map
Combined ALBERT Sheet.   Appendix 1.   Copy No. 9.

1.   The Bn. will entrain at MERICOURT L'ABBE tomorrow 8th inst., to proceed to ARQUES LA BATAILLE.

2.   Bn. H.Qrs. and "C" & "D" Coys. will proceed by first train leaving at 1.0 p.m.

       "A" & "B" Coys. by second train leaving at 4.0 p.m. O.C. 2nd train :- Major C.J. BROOKES.

3.   **1st Train.**

       Time of Parade :-   Transport 9.45 a.m.
                                     Personnel 12. 0 noon.

       2nd Train :-

       Time of Parade :-   Transport 1. 0 p.m.
                                     Personnel 3. 0 p.m.

       Place of Parade - Station yard (north side of Station.)

4.   Coys. Orderly Officers of "C" & "D" Coys., will report to the Adjutant on station at 12 noon.

5.   "A" & "B" Coys. will each provide a loading party of 1 Officer and 25 N.C.O's and men who will parade at the Station yard at 9.45 A.m. and report to Lt. C.V. FORSLIND, M.C., and carry out the loading for the whole Bn.

6.   Bn. H.Qrs. transport will be divided between the trains as follows :-

       1st Train: 3 G.S. Waggons;   1 Water Cart;   1 Limber;
                       1 Mess Cart.
       2nd Train: 3 G.S. Waggons;   2 Limbers.

7.   Coys. will render entraining states in duplicate at 11.0 a.m.

8.   Every effort will be made to leave the billets in as clean a state as possible

9.   ACKNOWLEDGE.

Issued at   p.m.   Capt. & Adjt.
7th September, 1918.   50th Bn. M.G.Corps.

Copies to :-

1.   C. O.
2.   "A" Coy.
3.   "B" Coy.
4.   "C" Coy.
5.   "D" Coy.
6.   Qr. Mr.
7.   Lt. C.V. Forslind, M.C.
8.   War Diary.
9.   " "
10.   File.
11.   "
12.   R.T.O.
13.   M.O.

Ref: 1/100,000 Maps
DIEPPE & LENS.

50th Bn. M.G.C. ORDER No. 22. 23
Appendix 2

SECRET.
Copy No. 14.

1. The Bn. will move by rail from ROUXMESNIL to DOULLENS tomorrow 16th inst., and on arrival will concentrate in the LUCHEUX area.

2. Parades and Entraining will be carried out in accordance with attached schedule.

3. ENTRAINING OFFICER will obtain from Bn. Orderly Room at 10.0 a.m. the entraining states for both trains and will arrange entraining for both trains. He will report to the R.T.O. one hour before loading time in each case and obtain permission from the R.T.O. for the troops to enter the Station. He will assist to supervise loading of vehicles, etc.
He will proceed by the second train.

4. Loading and unloading parties will contain a proportion of men who have done similar work before.
The same party will work on both trains

5. The Detraining Officer will proceed by the 1st train and on arrival will immediately report to the R.T.O. DOULLENS.

6. A Billeting Party of 1 N.C.O. (mounted on a bicycle) per Coy. and Bn. H.Q. will report to 2nd Lt. W.H.DOUCHE at 5.0 p.m. today at Bn. Orderly Room, and will proceed by 6.36 train this evening with the 2nd N.Fus. On arrival at DOULLENS 2nd Lt. W.H.DOUCHE will report to the R.T.O. for instructions as to billeting area, etc.

7. O.C. "D" & "Q" Coys. will detail a picquet on their trains to see that all doors on the right side of the train are kept shut, and that troops do not leave the train except at recognised "Halte Repas" or under orders of O.C. Trains.

8. All animals will be watered before leaving MARTIN EGLISE.

9. Water carts will be filled before loading.

10. RATIONS as follows will be carried:- On the man :- Unconsumed portions of rations for 16th.
On Transport;- Rations for 17th.
Rations for 18th inst. will be delivered in the new area.

11. Weather permitting "B" & "C" Coys. will be clear of the camp and standing by on the ground below the camp one hour before parade time. O's C. "B" & "C" Coys. will detail parties of 1 Officer and 25 O.R. to clean the camp thoroughly before leaving. (These parties will be detailed whatever the weather may be.)

12. All Tables, Forms, fire buckets, will be stacked at the Bn. Qr.Mr. Stores at 10.0 a.m. O.C. Coys. will detail a working party of 1 N.C.O. and 8 men per Coy. to report to the Qr.Mr. at 10.0 a.m.

13. Entraining states on the attached form (forwarded to Coys. only) will be forwarded to Bn. Orderly Room at 9.0 a.m. 16.9.18.

Issued at 6.15 p.m.
15th September, 1918.

A Denny
Capt. & Adjt.
50th Bn. M.G.Corps.

1. C.O.
2. "A" Coy.
3. "B" Coy.
4. "C" Coy.
5. "D" Coy.
6. Qr.Mr.
7. Major J. Morris, DSO.
8. 2nd Lt. W.H. Douche.
9. 2nd Lt. W.M. Gray.
10. Lt. C.I. Peacock.
11. R.T.O. ROUXMESNIL.
12. Camp Commandant.
13. War Diary.
14. " "
15. File.

SCHEDULE with ORDER No. 23

Train No.	CONTENTS.	Loading time. Time of Departure.	Loading time. Transport.	Loading time. Personnel.	Time of Parade. Main road below Camp. Transport.	Time of Parade. Main road below Camp. Personnel.	O.C. Train.	Entraining Officer.	Detraining Officer.	Loading Party.	Unloading Party.
1.	"A" & "D" Coys complete. (1 Coy. R.I.R. with Cooker & Team). Bn. H.Q. 37 N.C.O. & Men. 1½ vehicles.	4.16 p.m.	1.15 p.m.	3.15 p.m.	12.15 p.m.	2.15 pm.	Major C.J.BROOKES	2nd Lieut. W.H.GRAY.	Lieut. C.I.PEACOCK	1 Officer 25 NCO's and men from each of "B" & "C" Coys.	1 Officer 25 NCO's & men from each of "A" & "D" Coys.
2.	"B" & "C" Coys remainder of Bn. H.Qrs.	6.56 pm.	3.56 pm.	5.56 pm.	2.50 pm.	4.50 pm.	Major J. NORRIS, D.S.O.	Do.	Do.	do.	do.

15th September, 1918.

Capt. & Adjt.
50th Bn. M.G.Corps.

Reference
1/100,000 Maps
Sheet 17 (& 11) ?   50th Bn. M.G.C. ORDER No. 24.

SECRET.

Copy No. 9

Append 3

MOVE. 1. The Bn. Transport will move to the MEAULTE Sub Area today.

RENDEZVOUS 2. The transport of "B" & "C" Coys. and Bn. H.Q. will rendezvous on the St. GRATIEN - QUERRIEU Road. Head of column 300 yards S.E. of Bn. H.Q., and will move off at 11.15 a.m. The transport of "A" & "D" Coys. will rendezvous at 11.0 a.m. on the road running south from S.W. corner of FRECHENCOURT. Head of column 100 yards short of road junction immediately North of last U in QUERRIEU and will join column in rear of Bn. H.Q. as the latter passes.

ORDER of MARCH. 3. "B" Coy; "C" Coy; Bn. H.Q., "D" Coy; "A" Coy.

ROUTE. 4. QUERRIEU - LA HOUSSOYE cross roads S.E. of FRANVILLERS - HEILLY - BUIRE-sur-l'ANCRE.

COMMAND. 5. Lt. C. WOOD will be in command of the Bn. Transport. 151st Inf. Bde. will detail a field Officer to command the whole Divisional transport.

INTERVALS. 6. Intervals will be observed as follows :-
50 yds. between sections of 12 vehicles.
800 yds. between this unit and other units.

BRAKESMEN. 7. A Brakesman will march in rear of each vehicle.

HALTS. 8. Column will halt for 1½ hours at 1. 0 p.m.

WATER. 9. Water is not available on the road and must be carried.

BILLETING PARTIES. 10. A N.C.O. mounted on cycle from each Coy. and Bn. H.Q. will report to 2nd Lt. W.H. DOUCHE at Bn. H.Q. at 10.0 a.m. This billeting party will proceed to report to a Div.Staff Officer at the cross roads one mile west of first L in Le CARCAILLOT.

COOKING. 11. Dixies required for dinners and teas will be retained by Coys. and sent to Bn. Qr.Mr. Stores whence they will be carried by lorry to destination of Bn.

PACKS & BLANKETS. 12. Packs and blankets will be retained and taken by bus.

BICYCLES. 13. One bicycle per Coy. and 2 for Bn. H.Q. will be retained. The remainder will go with transport.

SUPPLIES 14. Normal.

LORRIES 15. O.C. Coys. will notify the Adjutant immediately of any accomodation for carrying kit, etc., they may require in the two lorries allotted to this Bn.

Issued at 9.15 a.m.
27th September, 1918.
Issued Copies to :-
1. C.O.
2. "A" Coy.
3. "B" Coy.
4. "C" Coy.
5. "D" Coy.
6. Qr. Mr.
7. 2nd Lt. W.H. DOUCHE.
8. Lt. C. Wood.
9 & 10. War Diary.
11. File.

A Denis
Major.
Adjt. 50th Bn. M.G.Corps.

Reference:
1/100,000 Maps
Sheets 11 & 17.   50th Bn. M.G.C. ORDER No. 25.   SECRET.
                                                          Copy No. 1?
                                         Appendix 1.

MOVE   1.(a) The personnel of the Bn. will move by bus today from the
               St. GRATIEN - BEAUCOURT road to MOISLAINS in III Corps area.

        (b)   Battle Surplus will move to POULAINVILLE by march route.

        (c)   Personnel of Divisional School will move to ALLONVILLE by
               march route.

        (d)   The Bn. Transport will rejoin the Bn. at MOISLAINS under
               orders of the Divn.

PARADES 2.   "A" & "D" Coys. parade on FRECHENCOURT - MONTIGNY (4th Class)
               Road.
               Head of Column on outskirts of FRECHENCOURT.
               Time of Starting - 12.20 p.m.
               and will march under command of Major C.J. BROOKS to cross roads
               1/3rd mile N.W. of MONTIGNY (facing N.E.)
               Bn. H.Q., "B" & "C" Coys. will parade on the road running
               north from St. GRATIEN.
               Head of Column at Cross roads ½ mile N. of St. GRATIEN.
               Order of March - Bn. H.Q., "C" Coy; "B" Coy.
               Time of Starting - 12.20 p.m.
               and will march to cross roads 1/3rd mile N.W. of MONTIGNY,
               halting in rear of "A" & "D" Coys.

NUMBER FOR   Personnel will be told off into parties of 25 before leaving
Each Bus. 3.   Coy. parade ground and on arrival at embussing point will
               keep clear of the road as far as possible.

OFFICER in   Capt. J.H. MIDDLETON will proceed in advance to the same
ADVANCE. 4.   rendezvous and ascertain all particulars regarding embussing
               of this Bn. and of 5th R.I.R. (?)

DIVNL. SIGNALLING   Personnel detailed for Divnl. Signalling Course will
COURSE. 5.   report to Adjutant at 11.0 a.m. at Bn. H.Q. They will
                    be in possession of tomorrows rations and will carry their blankets
                    and packs.

BATTLE   The Battle Surplus of all Coys. will parade on road outside
SURPLUS 6.   Bn. H.Q. at 1.0 p.m. facing west and will be ready to march
               off. They will be in possession of unexpired portion of the
               days rations and will carry their packs.

LORRIES for   All Cooking utensils, Officers' mess baskets etc., which
Forward AREA. 7. are required to be taken to forward area by lorry will
               be at Qr.Mr.Stores at 10.0 a.m.

LORRIES for   The blankets, Officers' kits, cooking utensils, etc.,
BATTLE SURPLUS. 8. of the battle surplus will be at the Q.M.Stores at
               10.0 a.m. and will be conveyed by lorry to their des-
               tination.
                                                        Major.
Issued at 9.15 a.m.   Adjt. 50th Bn. M.G.Corps.
28th September, 1918.
Copies to :-
1.   C.O.
2.   "A" Coy.
3.   "B" Coy.
4.   "C" Coy.
5.   "D" Coy.
6.   Qr.Mr.
7.   Major Morris, D.S.O. Lt G. REAH
8.   Lt. A.H.Morrison.
9.   M.O.
10. R.S.M.
11 & 12. War Diary.
13. File.
14   Capt. J.H. Middleton.

Confidential.

Volume VII.

War Diary of 50th. Bn. M.G.C.

From Oct. 1st 1918.
To   Oct 31st 1918.

WAR DIARY or INTELLIGENCE SUMMARY

Army Form C. 2118.

Place	Date	Hour	Summary of Events and Information	Remarks and references to Appendices
At rest	1st Oct		Weather very fair. Mobile bns. ordered hrs. ordered fortnight 30/10	Appendix 2
billets	2nd		Breakfast, unsettled, rain at intervals	
	3rd		Weather fair & cold. Casualties Capt C.H.M Toy wounded, 30 OR 0.0.2 so received	Appendix 3
	4th		Weather fair. Casualties 1 OR killed, 12 OR wounded, 50 M.G. Ptes. W.O.4	Appendix 4
	5th		Weather unsettled, rain at intervals, Casualties 6 OR wounded	C/4
	6th		Weather fair all day. Casualties Nil	C/4
	7th			
			Weather rain at intervals. Bn. Order No 26 issued. 2 Lt. J.H. HARVIE wounded, 2 OR killed.	Appx Nos
			4 OR wounded	C/4 Appendix 6
	8th		Weather unsettled. Casualties 11 OR wounded. Bn. Order No 29 issued.	C/4
At rest	9th		Weather fine in evening. Rain in afternoon.	C/4
At rest	10th		Weather dull in morning fine in afternoon	C/4
In the line	11th		Weather fair rain at intervals. A draft of 21 O.R. arrived from M.G. Base.	C/4
	12th		Weather unsettled. Draft. Casualties 4 O.R. killed, 4 O.R. wounded.	C/4
	13th		Weather fair. Unsettled – fine. Casualties 1 O.R. killed, 2 O.R. wounded	C/4
	14th		Weather very light rainfall. Casualties 2 O.R. killed, 13 O.R. wounded	C/4
			Bn Order no 30 issued. Amendment issued	C/4 after

Appendix No 1 Narrative 1st – 19th October

Albany Roy

WAR DIARY or INTELLIGENCE SUMMARY

Army Form C. 2118.

Place	Date	Hour	Summary of Events and Information	Remarks and references to Appendices
Inchy	15th		Weather very bright. Battalion forming Cavalier. 1 OR wounded. Preliminary bombardment started.	Appx 8. 2/9/Six.8.
	16		Weather dull & warm part of day, Bn in same area. No 31 & 2 drawn issued.	Appx No 9 2 No 1 No 17th
	17		Foggy early, very heavy strong enemy fire on all lines. Bn. O.R.s M.32 wounded. Casualties:-	Appx No 10
			2/Lt. A. HANCOCK killed. 12 OR killed, 2/Lt. S. MACHIN, 2/Lt. SAM. KEELER, 2/Lt. A. H. RODGERS wounded. 50 OR wounded. Bn Order No 16	
	18		Very fine all day. Casualties 2 OR killed, 6 OR wounded	Appx No 11 OR
	19		Broken fine all day. Bn Order No 33 issued	
	20th		Bn. HQ to "A" Coy moved from HENNECHY to MARETZ arriving at MARETZ at 12.00. Col CHARTERIS visited the Bn. C.O. attended	Appx No 12
	21st		conference at 2.5th Divn H.Q. Rained all day. O.C. 13 - C.Coy. reconnoitered the line. Bn Order No 34 issued. 5 officers rein. for cements arrived from M.G. Base Depot. for battalions	OR
	22		C.O., O.C. 13 & C.Coys reconnoitered the line in morning. B & C Coys proceeded up the line at 13.15. Bn H.Q. the Chateau le CATEAU. STATION Draft of 2 officers and 117 OR arrived from M.G. Base. Rain most of day	OR

A Smyth

WAR DIARY or INTELLIGENCE SUMMARY

Army Form C. 2118.

(Erase heading not required.)

Place	Date	Hour	Summary of Events and Information	Remarks and references to Appendices
	23rd		Bn. Comdr. received the offensive Bn. & Coy. attached to 25th M.G.B. Look out Battery position in O5058 and O6442. Ref Brigade No. 34. Tasks were carried out as laid down in this order. ZERO 01.20 hours. 13th C. Coy. were withdrawn from the line at about 10.00 hours, and rejoined the Bn. at MARETZ. Casualties. Killed 12nd A.O. CRUICKSHANK & F.C.R. Wounded 2/Lt N.M. STEEL & 16 O.R. Join in moving dux at intervals in afternoon.	Offensive Ms 12 OO4
	24		C.O. and Major PASTEUR attended cent of enquiry at 149 Bn. H.Q. C. Coy has both buttes fair.	OO4
	25th		G.O.C. 50th Div. umpires the Bn. and presents reffens to A.C.O's when C.O. inspected Draft in afternoon. C.O.'s conference Course started for N.C.O's of infantry battalion of the Division an arrive of the German machine gun.	OO4
	26th		C.O. Confines with G.O.C. 50th Div. and later went on leave to Paris.	OO4
	27th		A.I.R. P. Coy. has letter. Draft of 20 O.R. arrived. breakfast from Church Parade. Join in morning. rain during the afternoon. A.Derryhay.	OO4

WAR DIARY
or
INTELLIGENCE SUMMARY

(Erase heading not required.)

Army Form C. 2118.

Place	Date	Hour	Summary of Events and Information	Remarks and references to Appendices
	28th		O.C. Coys attended conference with G.O.C' Brigade. 2nd W.S. H.W.O.E joined Bn	O/4 Appendix No 13
	29th		Bn. Bne M.E Base. Fair all day.	
			Rfts Per Bn no 35. Bn. moved from MARETZ to LE CATEAU arriving at LE CATEAU at 14.30. One Officer + 25 O.R. arrived from M.E. Base. Fine all day. Received 50th Div. Operation Order no 260.	O/T
	30th		# Coy for the relief of Battn. of 18th + 25th Divs.	O/T
			A Coy went into line with 150th Bde. relieving 6 Jun. 25th An. G.132.	
			+ B Coy. 18th M.G. Bn. 2 in Co. A. H in G.I.D. + two Guns in reserve at Coy H.Q. located at L'HILACE	
	31st		Major Dering attended Conference at Div H.Q. Situation	O/T
			on Bn. front normal, weather fine.	
			Casualties for month off	
			O.R.	
			2 killed 32 killed	
			1 died of wounds 2 missing	
			wounded 126 wounded	

Aden Grey

APPENDIX V

SECRET.
Copy No. 10.

204th. Bn., M.G.C.

ORDER No. 5.

RELIEF. (1). - D Coy. will relieve B Coy. in the left sub-section on the night 25th./26th. May, 1918.
Relief will be completed by 6.0 a.m. on May 26th., at which hour O.C., D Coy. will take over command of the Machine Guns in the left sub-section.
Details of relief will be arranged between Coy. Commanders concerned.

REPORT. (2). - Completion of relief will be reported by wire by the code word - "HUBA".

DUTIES (3). - On completion of relief B Coy. will proceed to ON huts in Transport Lines at MAIZY, and will take over all
RELIEF. orders and find all working parties detailed to the Coy. in Divisional Reserve.

[signature] Capt.. & Adjt..

26th. MAY, 1918.

204th. Bn., M.G.C..

Copies to :-

(1). - Commanding Officer.
(2). - O.C., A Coy..
(3). - "   " B "
(4). - "   " C "
(5). - "   " D "
(6). - Quartermaster.
(7). - Medical Officer.
(8). - 150th. Inf. Bde..
(9). - War Diary.
(10). - "
(11). - File.

50th Battalion M. G. C.

NARRATIVE of OPERATIONS 27th - 29th MAY.

At midnight 26th-27th May the front of the 50th Division was held by 88 Vickers Guns, together with eight St. Etienne guns, four on the CRAONNE-LA HUTTE switch and four on the high ground near CRAONNELLE, manned by French Territorial troops.

Hostile artillery opened at 1 a.m. on the 27th on the whole of the Divisional front. Gas shelling was severe locally - more especially in the neighbourhood of the BUTTE de L'EDMOND, PLATEAU de CALIFORNIE and P.C. TERRASSE. In the centre subsection it was not necessary to wear gas helmets, but the bombardment by 5.9, and 4.2 with instantanious fuze, was very heavy, only one gun remaining in action, N. of the BUTTE DES PINS, at the moment of attack.

From 1 a.m. to 4 a.m. harrassing fire was carried out by all available guns on the enemy's tracks and communications. The attack was launched at 4.20 a.m. under cover of the cloud produced by gas shells. Dealing with the situation from right to left, six tanks preceded the attack on the right and eight guns were put out of action by them after having fired about 10000 rounds at infantry and tanks. These guns were located as follows. Two in Tr. de MARGRAVE, three in Tr. de DARDANELLES and three in BASTION de ROTTERDAM. One gun in the latter position remained in action until a tank was within 40 yards, when it was successfully withdrawn by L/C POND, only to be destroyed during the subsequent fighting.

Four guns at the BUTTE de L'EDMOND were knocked out by direct hits previous to the attack; their teams were much affected by gas and suffered very heavy casualties from shell fire.

The four reserve guns were all destroyed by the enemy barrage on the way to Coy. H.Q.

Four guns in the neighbourhood of Coy. H.Q. were successfully withdrawn and fought a rear guard action. Two were put out of action near PONTAVERT Cemetery owing to every man in the gun team being a casualty. Two held the Canal Bridge at CONCEVREUX for half an hour when they were also put out of action by direct hits.

Major Dawburn + Captain C.V. FORSLIND was wounded near this point successfully withdrew about 30 men, who ultimately fought as riflemen with details of the 6th D.L.I. & other units.

In the centre subsection gas shelling does not appear to have been heavy except in the neighbourhood of Le HUTTE. Artillery fire, 5.9 and 4.2, was, however, very intense, and very few guns survived the preliminary bombardment. It must be borne in mind that all available guns were firing on S.O.S. lines.

Three guns in the neighbourhood of the BUTTE des PINS did remain in action until completely shot out of ammunition, and appear to have inflicted considerable loss. Any guns surviving in front of the redoubt line appear to have been surrounded from the East, and none of the personnel has returned.

In the left subsection shelling both by H.E. and gas shells was very heavy, about 50% of the shells being gas. No serious frontal attack was made, the whole of the PLATEAU de CALIFORNIE being turned from either flank. Gun teams on the forward slope engaged a skirmishing line on their front and had no knowledge that the position was turned and their line of withdrawal cut off. Only three or four guns appear to have survived the preliminary bombardment, while firing themselves on S.O.S. lines. The enemy appears to have reached La HUTTE much at the same time as the PLATEAU de CALIFORNIE.

The reserve Company had no chance of coming into action. A very heavy bombardment both by gas shelling and H.E. was maintained on P.C. TERRASSE until it was cut off by converging movements from the direction of le BLANC SABLON Chateau and CRAONNELLE; only two men managed to return, one of whom escaped after being made a prisoner. There were many casualties both from gas and shell fire.

After the enemy had reached BEAURIEUX four out of eight guns for whom personnel had, fortunately, not been available for the line were got into action on the high ground S. of the AISNE ½ mile E. of MAIZY. They found excellent targets on columns advancing infile towards the bridges, and caused very considerable casualties. Two mounted officers were seen to fall and the enemy were held up for a period of an hour. It was not mot until the position was turned by the enemy advancing on the east through MAIZY that the survivors withdrew. One gun though damaged by M.G. fire was withdrawn and fought a rearguard action as far as the high ground N. of BARLIEUX, when the detachment succeeded in holding up the enemy for half an hour. The gun was then destroyed by a shell, and the few survivors passed back through some French troops to rejoin what remained of the Battalion near FISMES. Throughout its withdrawal this detachment was entirely isolated, and fought with great determination.

Machine gun and artillery fire was very severe, eight limbers and nineteen animals being destroyed on the Battalion waggon lines adjoining the positions held.

No touch could be established with Divisional H.Q. but at about 6.0 p.m. a verbal message was received that the Battalion was to concentrate at CRUGNY. It arrived there at about 8.0 p.m.

Early the following morning a verbal message was received that the Battalion was to proceed to BROUILLET and await orders. The village was reached at noon, but touch could not be established with Divisional Headquarters. It lies in a hollow, and was constantly being reconnoitred by hostile aeroplanes.

Accordingly at 5.30 p.m. as no orders had been received, and there appeared to be no troops in the neighbourhood, the Battalion took up a line on the high ground near the BOIS de 5 PILLES. GUNS and posts were mounted, and the transport bivouacked at the N. of the BOIS de REIMS. A report came to hand that Divisional H.Q. were established at LAGERY. It was found, however, that the 15th French Division was just arriving at this village, and the Battalion was placed at the disposal of the Divisional Commander. Four guns and 100 riflemen with 16000 rounds of ammunition in all stiffened the French line in the BOIS DORMONT.

The night passed quietly, apart from a little Machine Gun fire, but at dawn the enemy made a strong attack in a thick mist with Machine Guns and Minenwerfers. Two guns fired all their ammunition with very satisfactory results. The remainder kept in action until the French Commander and other officers and men were wounded, when it was decided to withdraw the line about 1200 yards to the B. de LHERY.

This was successfully accomplished and at about 10.0 a.m. the enemy, apart from any desultory M.G. fire, shewed no signs of further activity it was decided to reoccupy BOIS DORMONT.

This was done, and two very exhausted prisoners were captured. Shortly after 3 p.m. orders were received for the Battalion to rejoin the Division at IGNY le JARD, S. of the MARNE, where it arrived early on the morning of May 30th.

2nd June, 1918.

Lieut. Col.
Commdg. 50th M.G.Bn.

Corrigenda No.1 to 50th Battn M.G.Corps'
    Order No.7.
    ──────────

    The Battn will stage night of 1/2nd July in
LINTHELLES.

1-6-18.

                                     Capt and Adj.
                              50th Battn M.G.Corps.

Copies to all
recipients of Order No.7.

MARCH TABLE to ACCOMPANY 50th Bn. M.G.CORPS ORDER NO. 7.

Coy.	Date.	Move to	Starting Point.	Time of passing Starting Point.
H.Q.	1st July.	LINTHELLES.	Main entrance to CHATEAU on the SOIZY-aux-BOIS — SEZANNE road.	2.50 p.m.
"A"	"	"	"	2.53 p.m.
"B"	"	"	"	2.36 p.m.
"C"	"	"	"	2.39 p.m.
"D"	"	"	"	2.42 p.m.

An interval of 50 yards will be maintained between each Company.

Transport will march as a Battalion with the exception of Cookers which will follow in rear of their respective Companies.

An interval of 25 yards will be maintained between every sixth vehicle.

Reference :-
Map Sheet 10 N.W. Europe.
1/250,000.

50th Battn. M.G. Corps. Order No. 7.   SECRET.

Copy No. 8.

MOVE. 1. Battalion will move to LINTHES tomorrow July 1st., at 2.30 p.m. in accordance with attached march table.

ADVANCED PARTIES. 2. One Officer per Company will meet 2nd Lt. W.H. DOUCHE at the Mairie LINTHES at 4.30 p.m.

PARADE STATES. 3. Parade States will be handed in to the Adjutant before the Battalion moves off.

SANITATION 4. Company Commanders will ensure that all Billets and bivouac areas are left in a scrupulously clean condition and that all Latrines are filled in and rubbish destroyed, and will render a certificate to this effect by 2.0 p.m. tomorrow.

CLAIMS. 5. All claims for damage will be rendered to Battalion Headquarters by 10.0 a.m.

DRINKING ON LINE OF MARCH. 6. Company Commanders will be held responsible that the standing order with regard to drinking on the line of march or during halts is strictly observed.

TEAS. 7. Teas will be served at the third halt. The Battalion will move off again at 5.30 p.m.

Issued at 4.0 p.m.
30th June, 1918.

Capt. A. Adjt.
50th Bn. M.G. Corps.

Copies to :-
1 Commanding Officer.
2 A Company.
3 B Company.
4 C Company.
5 D Company.
6 Transport Officer.
7 Q.M.
8 War Diary.
9
10
11 File.

Reference :-
1/40,000 Sheet 62c. &
1/20,000 Sheet MOISLAINS.

50th Bn. M.G.C. ORDER No. 28.

Appendix 2

SECRET.

Copy No. 12

DIVISIONAL
ENEMY. 1. The 50th Divn. will relieve the 18th Divn. in the line today.
140th Bde. will hold Divnl. front on a 2 Bn. front. Bde. H.Q. will be at HAY COPSE (F.9.c.8.5.)
151st Bde. will be in support. Bde. H.Q. at F.1.b.0.7.
150th Bde. will be in reserve at NURLU.
S.A.A. Section 50th D.A.C. will be located in sandpit at D.3.D.

M.G. Bn.
RELIEF. 2. "B" & "D" Coys. will relieve Coys. of the 18th Bn. in the front line.
"A" Coy. will be in support.
"C" Coy. will be in reserve.
Details of relief will be arranged between Coys. concerned.

MOVE. 3. The Bn. will parade on the road MOISLAINS - NURLU (running through D.8.b.) facing East and will move off at 14.30.
DRESS - Fighting Order with greatcoats strapped on belts at back.
Starting Point. 350 yards short of cross roads at D.4.c.5.8.
Order of March. "B" Coy; "D" Coy; "A" Coy; Bn. H.Q.; "C" Coy.
Coy. transport will march in rear of its own Company, and Bn. H.Q. transport in rear of Bn. H.Q.
The following intervals will be allowed on the Bn. moving off :-
Between Coys. - 100 yards.
Between a Coy. and its transport - 100 yards.
Between sections of 6 vehicles - 25 yards.
On reaching EPEHY the following additional intervals will be allowed :-
Between sections (Personnel) 50 yards.
ROUTE - NURLU, LIERAMONT, SAULCOURT, EPEHY.
ORDERLY OFFICER. O.C. Coys. will send a mounted orderly officer and one cyclist to march at the head of the column.

LOCATIONS of
H.Qrs. 4. Further orders will be issued later as to location of Bn. Advanced and Rear H.Qrs. and Coy. Advanced and Rear H.Q.

Issued at 12.40
1st October, 1918.
Copies to :-
1. C.O.
2. "A" Coy.
3. "B" Coy.
4. "C" Coy.
5. "D" Coy.
6. Maj. J. Morris, DSO.
7. Signal Officer.
8. 2nd Lt. W.H.Douche.
9. Qr.Mr.
10. R.S.M.
11 & 12. War Diary.
13. File.

Major.
Adjt. 50th Bn. M.G.Corps.

50th Bn. MACHINE GUN CORPS.

Narrative of Recent Operations.

Maps
MONTBREHAIN
1/20,000.

Appendix No 1

On the morning of the 1st October Bn. H.Q. moved from bivouacs near MOISLAINS to LIERAMONT in consequence of the relief by the 50th Divn. of the 18th Divn. "B" & "D" Coys. relieved two Coys. 18th M.G.Bn. on the general line X.29.a., F.6.a., A.2.b., "B" Coy. being on the right and "D" Coy. on the left, with Coy. H.Q. near RONSSOY WOOD and MAY COPSE respectively. "A" & "C" Coys. were bivouaced near RONSSOY WOOD. Two Australian Divns. had been much involved in clearing up the abortive attack by the American Corps on LE CATELET and GOUY and at 09.00 on the 2nd, orders were received to take over the front held by the Second Australian Divn., and a portion of the front of the 5th Australian Divn., from MONT ST. MARTIN to MACQUINCOURT Farm. At 10.00 the C.O. accompanied G.S.O.1 to visit the front and to make arrangements with the Australian Divns. concerned. Company Commanders were picked up at RONSSOY, but owing to the difficulty of locating the two Australian Divns. it was not until nearly 17.00 hrs., that arrangements could be completed. Eventually one section of "C" Coy. relieved independently two sections of the 5th Australian Divn. on the right, and "A" Coy., with one section "C" Coy., attached, relieved the 3rd Australian Divnl. front, with sections at A.15.d.9.2., A.9.d.4.0., A.9.c.9.9., A.2.d.7.3., and one section in reserve at SART FARM. Coy. H.Q. SART FARM, Bn. H.Q. were established at RONSSOY WOOD.

At about 20.00, orders were received that the Divn. would co-operate in the following morning in an attack by the 2nd Australian Divn., on the MASNIERES - BEAUREVOIR Line and would capture PROSPECT HILL, LE CATELET and GOUY. Attack to be carried out by 151st Inf. Bde., supported by one Coy. 50th Bn. M.G.Corps. At the same time one Bn. 149th Inf. Bde. was to capture and consolidate the high ground N.W. of LE CATELET. At this hour it was not possible to detail a complete Coy., as all Coys. were either in the line or carrying out a relief. Two sections in reserve in KNOLL Support were therefore withdrawn from "B" Coy., and placed under the command of O.C. "C" Coy.

The Commanding Officer arranged personally with G.O.C., 151st Inf. Bde. to attach one section to 6th Inniskillings who were attacking PROSPECT HILL, one section to the 4th Bn. K.R.R., and one section to the 1st K.O.Y.L.I., moving in support of the 4th K.R.R. to mop up GOUY and LE CATELET, one section being in reserve at Bde. H.Q.

The attack was launched at 06.00. Owing to the very short notice the section of M.G. attached to 1st K.O.Y.L.I. failed to arrive by Zero. The 6th Inniskillings did not reach their rendezvous and the attack on PROSPECT HILL was carried out by 1st K.O.Y.L.I. It was entirely successful in spite of the partial failure of the Australians, and of the attack on Le CATELET and the high ground N.W. of that place.

Capt. TOY, Commanding "C" Coy. was wounded very early in the day, and there was in consequence considerable loss of control.

The section attached to 4th K.R.R. could not keep up with the advance of that Bn., and failed to assist in the attack on LE CATELET, and was directed to positions in A.17.a. commanding the exits from GOUY.

The section in reserve at BONY was sent forward later in the day to the sunken road in A.17.c., while the sections attached to the Inniskillings and K.O.Y.L.I. established themselves on the LE CATELET Line, and in trench from A.16.a.9.9. to A.9.d.0.0.

One section of "C" Coy. in reserve to "A" Coy. was sent forward by G.O.C. 151st Inf. Bde. to BONY Pt. and the KNOB. He apparently was not aware that these positions were already strongly covered by fire.

The reserve section of "D" Coy. under 2nd Lt. BRANDRICK, was directed during the afternoon to defend the Eastern slopes of PROSPECT HILL and arrived in position during the evening.

During the night, 150th Inf. Bde. relieved 151st Inf. Bde. in the line, and at 06.10 on the morning of the 4th the attack on LE CATELET and the high ground in S.28 and S.29 was renewed under the orders of G.O.C., 150th Inf. Bde., with 1 Bn. 149th Inf. Bde. attd. The attack was supported by two sections "A" Coy. on the right, and one section "C" Coy. on the left. The attack on the right was completely successful and the section of machine guns on that flank were in position on PROSPECT HILL facing N.E. ten minutes after the infantry arrived. The second section having received no orders from the Inf. Bn. to which it was attached except to "follow along behind our reserve Coy." lost touch and finished up in the LE CATELET Line in A.17.a.

On the left the attack at first went equally well.

Subsequently, however, the Royal Fusiliers were driven back almost to their starting point, and the section of "C" Coy. co-operating with their attack, which had established itself in the front line N. of LE CATELET was compelled to withdraw.

Machine guns in the Hindenburg line had several excellent targets and report having killed a considerable number of the enemy.

The attack was renewed at dusk by the MUNSTER Fusiliers and 4th K.R.R.C., and the village of LE CATELET and the high ground in S.28 and S.29 finally captured and consolidated.

The left Bde. 50th Divn., was then relieved by a Bde. of the 38th Divn., and was able to reassume a one Bde. front.

By this time there was very great intermixture of Coys. and I re-organised my guns as follows :-

O.C. "A" Coy. took over command of the machine guns in the line with one section and 1 section "D" Coy. attached, on PROSPECT HILL, the remaining sections being in the LE CATELET Line, A.17.a. and c. Coy. H.Q. were established at BONY.

"B" Coy. held positions in A.2, A.3, A.9, A.10, and A.16.

"C" Coy. took over from "A" Coy. at A.15.d.9.1, A.9.d.6.2, one section remained in A.22.c, and the fourth section came into reserve at Coy. H.Q., SART FARM.

"D" Coys. dispositions remained unchanged.

At about midday on the 5th, verbal orders were received that an attack would be carried out on the BEAUREVOIR Line at dusk supported by an artillery and machine gun barrage.

O.C "A" Coy. was accordingly ordered to concentrate his guns on PROSPECT HILL and to establish his H.Q. in the sunken road in A.6.d. jointly with the O.C. attacking Bn. and an artillery liaison officer. This was carried out and 12000 rounds were fired. No liaison officer or Bn. Commander appeared, and the attack does not seem to have been carried out. The section of "D" Coy. attached was withdrawn and rejoined its own Coy.

During the afternoon orders were issued to concentrate all Coys, apart from Coy. on PROSPECT HILL and three sections "B" Coy. in the LE CATELET line, near BONY. This order was duly carried out and completion was reported by 21.00, officers and men bivouacking in the open in heavy rain.

An advanced report centre was established at the road junction A.14.d.9.2, connected up by wire to Bn. H.Q. and to Coys. and Coys. were held in readiness to move at any moment.

On the early morning of the 6th, I moved these Coys. into trenches and sunken roads in the vicinity and went up to PROSPECT HILL which I found strongly held by the guns of "A" Coy. On my return, as the outcome of a conference at Divnl. H.Q., at BONY, "D" Coy. was ordered to report to G.O.C. 149th Inf. Bde. at VAUXHALL QUARRY and moved off at about   occupying positions N. of GOUY, with Coy. H.Q. at GOUY. I moved H.Q. to a ravine about A.14.d.9.8. "B" & "C" Coys. were ordered to concentrate at LA PANNERIE SOUTH and moved off at about the same hour. O.C. "A" Coy., during the afternoon, in accordance with orders received from G.O.C. 150th Inf. Bde. moved two guns to GUIZANCOURT Farm, and endeavoured without success - the farm being still in German hands - to move a subsection to VILLERS Farm, and a section to a non-existant trench between that Farm abd GUIZANCOURT Farm.

On the afternoon of the 7th, "B" Coy. relieved "A" Coy. on PROSPECT HILL in preparation for an attack on the following day, and "C" Coy. moved forward in support to the sunken road in A.6.c, one section taking up a position on PROSPECT HILL. "A" Coy. was withdrawn to A.14.b, and all rear H.Q. moved forward to that neighbourhood.

During the morning, as a result of a Corps and Divnl. Conference, orders were issued for the attack, in conjunction with the 66th Divn. on the right and the 38th Divn. on the left, the role of the 50th Divn. being to form a defensive flank for the 66th Divn, South of VILLERS OUTREAUX, as far East as MARLICHES Farm and 17.c.

In order to facilitate this task the capture of VILLERS Farm, T.20.b. was carried out by the 1st K.O.Y.L.I. at 01.00 on the 8th, supported by 1 section "D" Coy. with complete success, about 50 prisoners being taken. An attack launched against VILLERS OUTREAUX by the 38th Divn. at the same hour from the north was held up by wire, and a Bn. of that Divn. endeavouring to attack that village from the south on the right of the 1st K.O.Y.L.I. lost its way and did nothing.

For the main attack, launched at 05.10 hrs. the Divnl. boundary on the right was GUIZANCOURT Farm, incl. T.27.cent., T.22.c.1.0, T.22.central and thence to MARLICHES Farm and on the left VILLERS Farm incl, T.21.B.0.8, T.16.c.0.0. T.1..a.0.0, and was carried out by the 4th Bn. K.R.R. with "B" Coy. 50th Bn. M.G.C. in support, with orders to mount batteries of a section each at T.26.a.9.9., T.21.d.5.0 and T.22. c.3.2. One section placed at the disposal of the Bn. Commander who ordered two guns to form a post near MARLICHES Farm in conjunction with one of his platoons. The remaining subsection was held in reserve. Sections moved in rear of the advancing Coys, and by 10.00 a defensive flank was satisfactorily established facing north. Two fine performances marked the advance. After forming a post at T.21.c.2.2, considerable machine gun fire was encountered from T.27.c., which held up the infantry's advance and made it impossible for the section of machine guns, detailed to establish a post at T.21.d.5.0, to move forward. Sergt. KELLY, section Sergt., succeeded in locating the enemy's position and at once dashed forward, followed by his section officer and two or three infantrymen. He and his officer, 2nd Lt. WELLER, arrived alone at the position after running 400 yards under M.G.fire and received the surrender of 4 officers, 47 men, 5 M.Guns, 2 light Minenwerfer and an anti-tank gun, thereby enabling the advance to continue. At a later stage in the operation the subsection of guns detailed to form a post near MARLICHES Farm, skilfully handled by 2nd Lt. W.M. GRAY, succeeded in obtaining superiority of fire over a German M.G. post and received the surrender of two guns and their teams.

This sub-section also had excellent targets on parties of Germans running from VILLERS OUTREAUX.

For some little time after the flank had been established the situation in the village was not clear, and at 10.00 I ordered "C" Coy. to establish a line of M.G.posts on PROSPECT HILL facing N.E. With the additional guns of "D" Coy. N. of VAUXHALL Quarry and at VILLERS Farm, any effective counter attack was quite impossible, and by noon the 38th Divn. succeeded in joining hands with the 66th Divn. at MARLICHES Farm, and the 50th Divn was pinched out.

Coys. were concentrated that night in the neighbourhood of BONY and moved to HARGIVAL Farm on the morning of the 9th October.

Casualties during that period amounted to 2 Officers, Capt. C.H.M. TOYm and 2nd Lt. J.H. HARVIE, wounded, and 3 O.R. killed and 33 wounded.

The main lesson to be learnt from these operations is the importance of receiving orders sufficiently soon to enable them to be carried out. Commanders had no opportunity to study their maps and no time to appreciate the vital orders issued. On broad lines machine gun co-operation on the 3rd October was a failure because it was a physical impossibility for guns to arrive at their destinations in time. On the 4th October more time was available and very considerable support was given to the attacking infantry, more especially by the stationary guns in the Hindenburg line N. of BONY. On the 8th October there was plenty of time to arrange all details, and from a M.G. point of view everything went well. Communications worked admirably and I was constantly in touch with the situation owing to the excellent reports sent in at definite hours by Major PASTEUR, M.C. Commanding "B" Coy.

Beyond this I am satisfied that it is far better when time permits to settle from the map, or with observation if possible, the approximate tasks of machine guns. The Inf. Bde. or Bn. Commander is very apt to forget in the stress of battle, the fire power of machine guns and their great value for the protection of a flank with fire - this does not mean that the guns themselves must necessarily be on the extreme edge of that flank - and I think one may say that sections placed at the disposal of Bn. Commanders without tasks previously allotted are hardly ever used to the best advantage. To a less but still considerable extent, the same criticism applies to the allocation of a Coy. to a Bde. If a Bde. is functioning as a complete unit, whether as an advanced guard or on detachment, this criticism does not, of course, apply, and a Coy. should invariably accompany it.

21st October, 1918.

Lieut. Colonel,
Commdg. 50th Bn. M.G.Corps.

Ref: Maps　　　50th Bn. MACHINE GUN CORPS　　　CONFIDENTIAL.
57b N.E. &
　　S.E.　　　NARRATIVE of OPERATIONS Oct.9th - 19th 1918.

On Oct. 9th the Bn. moved from the neighbourhood of BONY to bivouac in tents and shelters near HARGIVAL Farm. There was excellent water in the river and the Germans had left any quantity of material with which to construct shelters, and every one settled down very comfortably in anticipation of two or three days rest.

However at 13.30 hours, owing to the wonderful progress in the direction of LE CATEAU made by the 25th and 66th Divns., I was ordered to send a Coy. forthwith to join an advanced guard moving to SERAIN under the command of G.O.C. 150th Inf. Bde. and to be ready to move my Bn. at 14.00 to the same destination.

This warning order was subsequently cancelled and at 04.30 hours on the 10th., I received orders to move to HOMMECHY via GUIZANCOURT Farm, where I was informed as to the situation. The Bn. arrived at its destination at 16.15 hours and found excellent billets and a village almost uninjured by shell fire or Germans It was full of civilians who gave the troops a very cordial welcome. "D" Coy. proceeded to REUMONT and remained for the night under the command of G.O.C. 150th Inf. Bde.

On the 11th Oct. the Divn. relieved the 25th Divn., in the line, with an American Corps on the right and the 66th Divn., on the left. "D" Coy. took over somewhat indifferenct M.G. disp positions from the 100th Bn., who only had one section in the line. One section of "A" Coy. was attached to "D" Coy. in order to strengthen the M.G. defence.

On the afternoon of the 12th., as the result of a reconnaissance of the right of the Divnl. front, it appeared to me that the American dispositions were none too good and had no depth at all. I therefore put two additional sections of "A" Coy. into support positions at Q.20.a.central, P.25.central, P.24.c.6.6. All guns had a magnificient field of fire and effectively protected the right flank of the Divn.

During the night two guns of "D" Coy, badly sited at Q.20.a.6.3. were destroyed by shell fire, and on the following day after reconnoitring the left of the Divnl. sector, and after discussing the question with G.O.C. 150th Inf. Bde., guns were re-sited with a subsection at each of the following points :- Q.20.d.2.8;

Q.15.c.7.5; Q.9.a.8.2; Q.3.c.7.6; Q.8.d.5.5; Q.8.b.6.3; Q.2.d.2.3;
Q.13.b.0.3; Q.7.b.7.5; Q.2.c.2.6.   The guns covering the right
flank remain unchanged.

It had originally been intended to secure LE CATEAU and the
high ground east of the river SELLE on this day, but the crossing
of the river on the Divnl. front was found to present difficulties.
Accordingly on the 14th Oct., the 66th Divn. took over the front
approximately the far south the grid line Q.7.a.0.0; Q.8.a.0.0.
Q.9.a.0.0., and all guns N. of that line were relieved by guns of
the 25th M.G.Bn., during the evening with the exception of a subsection at Q.9.a.8.2., which that Bn. was not willing to relieve.
These guns were left in position to cover the bridge in Q.9.b.,
as at that time there was no infantry post holding it, and as G.O.C.
150th Inf. Bde. who was holding the line considered that guns were
required at that point.

O.C. "A" Coy. took command of all guns in the line after
relief and "D" Coy. withdrew to billets in R.UMONT, one section
being relieved by the remaining section of "A" Coy.   On the 15th
Oct. the Divn. took over a portion of the American front so as to
include a possible crossing of the River SELLE, N. of St. SOUPLET,
one section of "C" Coy. was attached to "A" Coy. relieved four
American guns and selected positions in Q.21.c., and Q.27.a. O.C.
"C" Coy. was ordered to hold his Coy. in readiness to move forward
to positions on the right in case of an enemy attack.

Orders were received that a general attack would be launched
by the Fourth Army on the morning of the 17th and that the 100th
M.G.Bn. would come under my orders for barrage purposes.   It was
accordingly arranged that 24 guns should take up battery positions
on the right of the Divnl. front., the remaining guns of the Bn.
being located on the high ground in Q.2. and Q.3., so as to barrage
the railway siding in Q.10, and the railway triangle in Q.5.

Later in the day one Coy. 18th BN. M.G.C. was placed at the
disposal of the Divn. for barrage purposes.   I therefore grouped
the whole of the 100th Bn., in Q.2, and Q.3, leaving to the 18th
Bn., positions in Q.27 and Q.28.   I arranged with O.C. 100th Bn.
the tasks of his Bn. including the relief of two guns of "A" Coy.
at Q.9.a.8.2, and instructed Major COX, commanding "D" Coy., to
reconnoitre positions for two 8 guns batteries of the 18th Bn.,
and to lay them out for specific targets.

Orders for the attack were issued with the following M.G. arrangements.

At Zero 98 guns - i.e., 16 guns 18th Bn. M.G.C., 56 guns 100th Bn. M.G.C., 16 guns "B" Coy. and 8 guns "C" Coy. were ordered to open fire on certain definite targets from battery positions. O.C. "D" Coy. with one section "C" Coy. attached was ordered to cross the river immediately in rear of the leading Bde. - 150th Inf. Bde., - and to take up battery positions in Q.28.b., in order to cover the right of 149th Inf. Bde., during its advance to the first objective - a line running approximately from R.13.d.5.3. to K.36.d.6.8. - and to detach one section to cover the re-entrant in R.17.central.

O.C. "A" Coy. was ordered to concentrate his Coy., and one section "C" Coy., attached, in the valley in Q.21.a. and c., and to move forward at Zero plus 30 mins., to battery positions in Q.10, and to concentrate on specific targets covering the left of the 149th Inf. Bde. O.C. "B" Coy. with two sections "C" Coy. attached, was ordered to move his group forward in rear of 150th Inf. Bde., and to establish battery positions to cover the advance of that Bde. to the final objective - the main road running from R.8.d.9.3., to LE CATEAU and to send two sections forward to assist in the consolidation of that line with special reference to the cross roads in R.3.a., and R.2.b., and the valley near J. JACQUES Mill in L.31.d.

All Coys. as soon as their barrage tasks were completed were ordered to consolidate in depth in the neighbourhood of their battery positions.

At about 02.00 on the 16th Oct. Major PATTERSON, commanding "D" Coy. 18th Bn. M.G.C., reported in person, and during the morning went round his proposed By. positions with 2nd Lt. BRANDRICK who had sited them.

During the day an advanced report centre was established at Q.19.d.75.83, connected to Coy. report centres at Q.20.d.3.9 (A Coy) Q.21.c.2.8. (B & C Coy. Group) Q.26.b.0.2. (D Coy & D Coy. 18th Bn. M.G.C.) H.Q. 100th Bn. M.G.C. and the advanced report centre of that Bn. at Q.2.d.0.0. were also connected by wire.

Owing to some mistake on the part of the traffic control "D" Coy. 18th Bn. M.G.C., which should have arrived at MAIROIS at 13.00 did not in fact arrive till 21.00. However, all the work had been done, and there was quite sufficient time to move the Coy. to its battery positions.

At Zero 06.10 on the 17th., all guns opened on their barrage lines and fired their allotted tasks with the exception of a battery in position S.W. of St. BENIN which suffered heavy casualties from shell fire and had to be withdrawn. The river was crossed without any great difficulty, but the morning was extremely misty, and the infantry found it impossible to keep touch or to locate pockets of the enemy during their advance, with the result that many small bodies of the enemy were passed over and had to be dealt with later. In consequence of the mist there was very great and inevitable delay and the whole of the 149th Inf. Bde. eventually became involved in the fight for the intermediate objective.

Dealing with the subsequent action of machine guns.

On the right three sections of "D" Coy. with one section "C" Coy., attached, moved forward in accordance with instructions to take up battery positions in Q.28, and to establish a section to cover the re-entrant in Q.17. Owing to the thick mist, gas, and a fairly heavy hostile barrage, there was considerable confusion at the river crossing, and the approaches were very much congested. Lieut. MEREDITH who was guiding the batteries, and who had reconnoitred a crossing nearer to St. BENIN during the night led them off the road and across the river by a bridge which had been blown up but remained passable.

The orderly sent to report to Major COX, who was leading the Coy., became a casualty en route, and after crossing the river and sending the section detailed to cover the re-entrant in Q.17 on its way under 2nd Lt. FRY, he found that the batteries were not behind. However, Lt. MEREDITH had led them successfully forward and established eight guns in battery positions whence they fired their allotted task. One gun was knocked out by shell fire together with its team, and the remainder lost their way and did not arrive till later. The situation was very obscure owing to the dense fog, and considerable enemy machine gun fire was coming from the left flank. After firing defensive positions were taken up in Q.28, Q.23, Q.22.

page 3. with his action

In the meantime 2nd Lt. FRY had pushed forward along the railway to about Q.22.c.7.6., where it was held up by M.G. fire from about Q.22.d.3.8. Having located the position he got his teams under cover and fetched a tank which disposed of the opposition. He then proceeded to the southern practice trench in Q.16.d., where he mounted his guns under heavy machine gun fire from the front and flank and trench mortar fire from the orchards. The fog was still very thick and no sign of our infantry could be seen. Accordingly Corpl. ROUTLEDGE and Cpl. McCURK volunteered to carry out a reconnaissance. They established the position of the enemy in the orchard in Q.17.a., and brought in a wounded man of the K.O.Y.L.I., from about 150 yds from the enemy, and eventually, at about 10.30 hours, located 2 officers and 16 O.R. K.O.Y.L.I. who had lost touch with their Bn., and had established themselves in the Practice trenches under heavy machine gun fire. Just at this time a party of the enemy with a white flag appeared through the hedge of the orchard; Lt. FRY got two guns into action and the enemy immediately replied killing one Sergt. and two Corporals. He at once pulled his two other guns into the open in order to enfilade the practise trenches to the north which the enemy were attempting to reach, and though the first two guns were knocked out, these two guns, together with rifle and Lewis gun fire from the small detachment of K.O.Y.L.I., who fought with great determination, succeeded in beating off the attack after fighting for some two hours. Lt. FRY then moved one gun to protect his right flank and at about 14.00 a party of Dublin Fusiliers advanced from the railway and occupied the road (intermediate objective) in Q.17.

During this time the situation on the right had not been very comfortable. The 4th K.R.R. who had been heavily shelled previous to zero, were driven back on the left by a strong counter attack near their point of junction with the 1st K.O.Y.L.I. At the request of the Officer commanding that Bn., two guns were sent out to support his right flank which was left in the air, and for a time things became quieter. However, at 13.45 the enemy again attacked 4th K.R.R. on their front and right flank and penetrated as far as the approximate line Q.29.b.9.9 - Q.23.c.central. This attack was broken up mainly by low flying aeroplanes and Lt. MEREDITH reports that his guns in Q.23.c. had good targets. The infantry re-occupied the intermediate objective.

They were again driven back at 17.30 and at 17.40 Lt. MEREDITH reported the line behind him on the high ground in Q.28.b. and d., and the receipt of verbal orders to conform to this movement on which he declined to act.

At 18.30 he reported that the 7th Wilts had gone through and had re-established the line of the intermediate objective, being in touch with the Americans near BANDIVAL Farm. He arranged with O.C. 7th Wilts an S.O.S. and flanking barrage and both he and 2nd Lt. FRY did conspicuously good work throughout the day. I was kept in constant touch with the situation by O.C "D" Coy., Major COX, who carried out during the course of the afternoon an admirable personal reconnaissance.

During the day O.C. "A" Coys. situation had been very difficult. His orders were to move forward at Zero plus plus 60 to the railway siding in Q.10 and to cover the left of 149t Inf. Bde., during its advance to the first objective. At Zero plus 45 mins., a patrol was sent forward to find out how the attack was progressing and at Zero plus 60 the Coy. moved off from its assembly position in Q.20.d. to the broken viaduct at Q.15.b.6.3. Shelling had been heavy during the advance and there were several casualties, including Lt. HANCOCK, killed. Twelve pack mules dumped 108 belt boxes at this point and returned for more. The teams made a bridge of sleepers and crossed the stream where they waited some time as there were no signs of any infantry. The Scottish Horse eventually reached the Embankment in Q.16.a., and teams pushed forward to join them, reporting to the Officer commanding that Bn., and at his request two sections were mounted in the embankment in Q.16.a. and c., firing towards the brickworks in Q.10.d., and two sections were mounted in Q.15.b., firing N.N.E.

During all this time there has been a dense mist, and it was almost impossible to get hold of the situation. The enemy had many machine guns in action which were firing from every direction. Two guns firing from the neighbourhood of CHAPEL BRIDGE MILLS were eventually put out of action, and our troops established themselves in the railway siding, but it was not until 17.00 that the infantry assaulted the Brickworks, Q.10.d The attack did not succeed. Machine gun covering fire was very difficult to arrange as section commanders were given no details of the attack by the infantry commanders on the spot. However, shortly after 21.00 the infantry were established throughout on the intermediate objective.

O.C. "B" Coy. experienced similar difficulties. After firing his barrage his orders were to concentrate his group and to report in person to G.O.C. 150th Inf. Bde. at QUENNELET GRANGE, Q.24.a. in order to co-operate in the attack of that Bde. on the second objective. At about 08.30 the Coy. Commander, Major PASTEUR, M.C., went forward to QUENNELET GRANGE, but ascertained on arriving at the sunken road in Q.23.a., that the situation had not developed according to plan, and succeeded after some little time in finding G.O.C. 150 Inf. Bde. in the embankment near St CREPIN, Q.28.a. In the meanwhile his guns, with the exception of the left battery, had crossed the river and had assembled near the railway bridge in Q.22.a. by 10.00. Soon after this, Major PASTEUR discovered that the bulk of our troops had fallen back to the line of the embankment, and that troops of the 150th Inf. Bde. would be utilized either to secure the intermediate objective, or, if the situation permitted, to take the first objective, and that the attack on the second objective would not take place. He accordingly mounted one section in the embankment to cover the ravine in Q.29.a. and Q.22.d., and withdrew the remainder in accordance with my orders, to a position of concentration S.W. of St. BENIN. I had also ordered the left battery, under Lieut. CRUIKSHANK, to arrange to cover Q.4.c., Q.9.b., and Q.10.a., and he therefore established his two sections at about Q.15.c.7.9. At about 17.00 it was decided to renew the attack on the following day, and I at once arranged the following M.G. co-operation.

O.C. "D" Coy. was ordered to barrage with a 5 gun battery the copse on the grid line between R.13 and Q.10 and to lift 300 yards at zero plus 20 minutes Fire to cease at zero plus 30 minutes. He was also ordered to hold two sections in readiness to move forward with the 75th Inf. Bde. to the second objective with the specific tasks of barraging as soon as possible the road junction at R.3.a.3.4. and R.2.b.4.6., and the neighbourhood of J.JACQUES Mill in L.31.d, and to consolidate in depth as soon as their tasks were accomplished.

O.C. "B" Coy. was ordered to barrage at Zero, Copse in Q.12.c., Practise trenches in Q.12.d., Copse on grid line between Q.11.a. and Q.12.a. At Zero plus 10 mins. all guns were ordered to lift 200 yards and at zero plus 20 mins., fire was ordered to cease, and two sections were ordered to move forward as soon as possible to assist in the consolidation of the first objective on the approximate front R.13.d.3.5. - R.7.a.central, with special regard to the right flank.

O.C. "A" Coy. was ordered to barrage the high ground on the line Q.12.central, Q.6.central and to lift at Zero plus 30 to the line R.7.a.0.0. R.1.a.0.0. At Zero plus 40 mins. all guns were ordered to cease fire and two sections were detailed to consolidate on the approximate front R.7.a.ct. - R.36.d.5.7. with special regard to the left flank.

The attack on the first objective was launched at 05.30 by three Composite Bdes. of the 50th Divn., with orders to consolidate it in depth. After a pause of two hours the 75th Inf. Bde. (25th Divn.) attached for the operation, were ordered to capture and consolidate the final objective.

All arrangements worked very satisfactorily, and at 08.30, O.C. "D" Coy. reported that his forward sections hade ceased fire and were consolidating in depth as the Dublin Fusiliers had pushed on to BAZUEL and had captured the final objective. On the left there was for some time heavy fighting in the railway triangle, but eventually it was clear of the enemy. An Officer of the North'd Fus. requested my section officer not to fire a barrage until his men were over the ridge as they were afraid of being hit in the back. He was assured that it was ~~perfectlysafe~~ perfevtly safe, and the barrage was duly fired, and it is satisfactory to not that later in the day several infantry men told him that though at first the sound of bullets overhead rather frightene them, it very soon gave them confidence, and got them forward. And they hoped, having found that they could "Stand up with safety"! that they would always have a machine gun barrage in future. During the fighting in the railway triangle two guns moved to the Sugar factory and Petroleum refinery to assist the Scottish Horse, one section reporting in person to the officer commanding that Bn.

Two guns were mounted at Q.10.b.5.7. to fire at the triangle, and two at Q.5.c.4.6. to fire acorss it. It was pointed out to O.C. Scottish Horse that owing to the great difficulty of ammunition supply it was not wise to snipe at individual Germans.

In the meantime O.C. "D" Coy. had been right through BAZUEL which he found to be clear of the enemy, and he was able to get some infantry, Gloucesters, forward in time to capture a battery of 4.2's and some artillery personnel who had returned to get them out of action.

2nd Lt. BRANDRICK utilized two German guns to protect th right flank of the 75th Bde. with great success, as the Americans at that time were some way back. At 14.00 as the situation on the right at LA ROUX Fme. was not very clear, I went up myself and found the farm strongly occupied with three American M.Gs. on a small ridge to the east of it, and the whole line was linked up and liaison established.

It could be seen that the German M.Gunners in the neighbourhood of LE QUENNELET GRANGE and the Orchards W. and N.W. of LA ROUX Farm, had put up a good fight, but by the time I got there, apart from very desultory and promiscuous shelling, and a burst of M.G. fire by the Americans at JONC DE MER Farm which elicited no reply that I could hear, the front was perfectly peaceful.

During the afternoon the 100th Bn. M.G.C. relieved "D" and "B" Coys. in the line, and established themselves on the flank LA ROUX FARM, LE QUENNELET GRANGE and on the high ground E. of the intermediate objective so as to dominate every possible counter attack from the direction of the railway triangle in Q.5.

One section was definitely detailed to form a strong point at LA ROUZ Farm.

On the morning of the 19th one Coy. 25th Bn. M.G.C. came up and took over from O.C. "A" Coy. who previously had been warned to hold his Coy. in readiness to move forward with an advanced guard under the command of G.O.C. 75th Inf. Bde. This advance did not materialize, and "A" Coy. returned to billets at HONNECHY, where Bn. H.Q. remained that night. The Divn. was relieved by the 25th Divn., and "B", "C" and "D" Coys. moved to billets at MARETZ.

From a machine gun point of view these operations were very satisfactory. There was ample time to get out orders and to study the ground, and although the fog on the morning of the 17th interfered considerably with our attack, communications were so admirably maintained that it was always possible to keep Coy. Commanders in touch with the situation. Liaison was good, and Coy. Commanders were continually in association with Bde. Commanders, either in person or by a liaison officer. It is still noticeable that infantry Bn. Commanders do not always appreciate that machine gun is not a bayonet, and that in order to defend a position it is not necessary or advisable to put machine guns in that position.

The use of limbers was difficult owing to the destruction of bridges, but pack mules were used right up to gun positions and the supply of rations, water and ammunition never failed. In the early stages a great deal of man handling was necessary, and it is impossible to speak too highly of the zeal and energy

page 10.

displayed by all ranks.

Maps are attached shewing tasks of barrage guns.

26th October, 1918.   Lieut. Colonel.
                              Commdg. 50th Bn. M.G.Corps.

CASUALTIES 9 - 12 Oct.

Killed   2/Lt. A. HANCOCK   27 O.R.

Wounded   2/Lt. A. H. RODGERS
          (since died of wounds)
          2/Lt. E.A.W. WELLER   16 O.R.
          Lieut. J.S. MACHIN
          Major C.J. BROOKS
          (at duty)

Missing   O.R. 2

Appendix No. 3

SECRET.

50th. DIVISION OPERATION ORDER No. 250.

1. The Scottish Horse will take over the whole of the Canal Line from the left of the Dublin Fusiliers in the Northern Divisional Boundary in S.19.c. under orders of G.O.C., 149th Brigade.

2. The Royal Fusiliers as soon as withdrawn and equipped with ammunition, tools, etc., will move to DUNCAN POST where they will be met by a guide who will conduct them to BONY.

3. On arrival at BONY the Battalion will come under the orders of the G.O.C., 150th Infantry Brigade, and will remain under his orders for the attack to-morrow morning.

4. The O.C., will come on in advance and will report at Divisional Headquarters, DUNCAN POST.

5. The Liaison Posts of the right flank of 53rd Division must be relieved and their flank Battalion be informed that the line is being thinned out.

6. One Reserve M.G. Section will be withdrawn from 149th Inf. Bde. and report to 150th Infantry Brigade at BONY, under orders to be issued by O.C., M.G. Battalion.

7. ACKNOWLEDGE.

Major for Lt.-Col,
General Staff,
50th. Division.

Issued at 19.40 hours.
3rd October, 1918.

Distribution :-

149th Infantry Brigade.
150th Infantry Brigade.
151st Infantry Brigade.
50th. Bn. M.G. Corps.

Reference Map
MONTBREHAIN
1/20,000.

50th Bn. M.G.C. ORDER No. 27.

SECRET.
Copy No 10

Appendix No 4.

The following relief will take place tonight :-

"A" Coy. will relieve "C" Coy. For the purposes of this relief one section of "D" Coy. under 2nd Lt. H. BRANDRICK, M.C. on PROSPECT HILL will remain in the line and will come under the command of O.C. "A" Coy.

Details of relief will be arranged between Coys. concerned.

O.C. "A" Coy. will establish his H.Q. at H.Q. 150th Inf. Bde. BONY. O.C. "C" Coy. taking over "A" Coys. H.Q. at SART FARM, F.17.a.5.6.

On completion of relief the following will be disposition of guns :-

"A" Company.

One section East of PROSPECT HILL. One section of "D" Coy. attached West of PROSPECT HILL. 3 Sections A.17.

"B" Company.

One section HIDDEN TRENCH A.2.b. 2 guns A.2.b.9.4. 2 guns A.3.c.1.0. 2 guns A.9.d.8.5. 2 guns A.16.a.9.9. One section in trench running from A.16.a.9.9. to A.10.c.0.0.

"C" Company.

One section relieve one section "A" Coy. A.15.d.9.1. One section relieve one section "A" Coy. A.9.d.6.2. One section in A.22.c. & d. one section in reserve at Coy. H.Q.

"D" Company.

One section attached to "A" Coy. om PROSPECT HILL. Remaining dispositions unaltered.

Issued at 16 hours.
4th October, 1918.

Major.
Adjt. 50th Bn. M. G. Corps.

Copies to :-

1. C.O.
2. "A" Coy.
3. "B" Coy.
4. "C" Coy.
5. "D" Coy.
6. 50th Divn. "G".
7. 149th Inf. Bde.
8. 150th Inf. Bde.
9. 151st Inf. Bde.
10. & 11. War Diary.
12. File.
13. Signalling Officer.
14. 2nd in Command.
15. Qr. Mr.

Reference Map 1/20,000 MONTBREHAIN.

50th Bn. M.G.C. ORDER No. 28.

Appendix No 5

SECRET.

Copy No. 14.

1. INFORMATION. In conjunction with other formations on the right and left the 50th Divn. will take part in an attack to be delivered at zero hour 8.10.18. The 66th Divn. is attacking on the right and the 38th Divn, 5th Corps. is attacking on the left.

2. BOUNDARIES. The Divnl. Boundary on the right - GUISANCOURT Farm incl. - T.27.central - T.22.c.1.0. - T.22.central, thence direct to MARLICHES Farm incl. On the left T.20.b.0.8. - VILIERS Farm incl. T.21.b.0.8. - T.16.c.0.0. - T.17.a.0.0.

3. OBJECTIVES. The role of the Divn. is to form a defensive flank for the 66th Divn. advancing on to their first objective from SONIA WOOD incl. through PETITE FOLIE Farm incl. - HAMAGE FARM incl. - MARLICHES Farm incl. at which point touch will be established with the 38th Divn.

4. DETAILED ORDERS TO TROOPS. The operation will consist of two phases, the attacks taking place at two different hours.
(1) At 01.00 hours the 38th Divn. will launch their attack on VILLERS OUTREAUX and at the same hour the SCOTTISH HORSE 149th Inf. Bde. will attack and capture VILIERS Farm from the south under a barrage. "D" Coy. 50th Bn. M.G.C. will co-operate in this attack under orders to be issued by G.O.C. 149th Inf. Bde.
(2) At a later hour - exact time will be notified to all concerned - 4th Bn. K.R.R., attached for the operation to 149th Inf. Bde., will establish a defensive flank as laid down in Order No. 3. "B" Coy., 50th Bn. M.G.C., will be attached to 149th Inf. Bde. for this operation and will mount batteries of one section each at about T.26.d.9.9. T.21.d.5.0. T.22.c.5.2. The remaining section will carry out any role required by O.C. 4th Bn. K.R.R., bearing in mind the importance of preventing any counter attack from a North easterly direction T. 10. & T.11.

It will be borne in mind that this attack will take place at a later hour than that launched by the 38th Divn. and that the role of troops is defensive and not offensive. Fire will therefore not be opened in a northern or north easterly direction except on observed enemy movement.

O.C. "B" Coy. will establish a rear H.Q. at about A.6.d.central by 17.00 hours today and will at once establish personal liaison with G.O.C. 149th Inf. Bde. at about A.11.b.0. He will also select a suitable report centre in or near the BEAUREVOIR Line, its location to be notified to Bn. H.Q. as soon as possible.

5. COMMUNICATION and REPORTS. O.C. Signal section will arrange to attach 4 cycle orderlies "B" Coy. for the operation. Progress reports will be sent back to Bn. H.Q. at A.14.b.9.8. at zero plus 2 hours, zero plus 4 hours and zero plus 6 hours.

Issued at 15.42hours.
7th October, 1918.
Copies to :-
1. O.C.
2. 2nd in Command.
3. Sig. Officer.
4. "A" Coy.
5. "B" Coy.
6. "C" Coy.
7. "D" Coy.
8. Qr. Mr.
9. 50th Divn. "G"
10. 38th Bn. M.G.C.
12. 66th Bn. M.G.C.
13. 149th Inf. Bde.
13 & 14. War Diary.
15. File.

Major
Adjt. 50th Bn. M.G.C.

Ref:
MAP MONTBREHAIN
1/20,000.

Appendix No 6

50th Bn. M.G.C. ORDER No. 29.

SECRET.
Copy No. 11

MOVE. 1. The Bn. will move to the HARGIVAL Farm area in C.2. and A.3. tomorrow.

PARADE 2. The personnel will march as a Bn. and the transport will move independently as Coys.
    Starting point:- Road junction A.9.a.7.5.
    Time of passing:- 11.00 hours.
    Order of March:- Bn. H.Q; "A" ; "C" ; "B" ; "D" Coys.

ADVANCE PARTY 3. O.C. Coys. will detail a party of one officer and 5 men to meet Major J. MORRIS, D.S.O. at the starting point at 00.30 hours.

Issued at 1815 hours.
8th October, 1918.

Major
Adjt. 50th Bn. M.G.Corps.

Copies to :-

1. C.O.
2. 2nd in Command.
3. Signalling Officer.
4. "A" Coy.
5. "B" Coy.
6. "C" Coy.
7. "D" Coy.
8. Qr. Mr.
9. 50th Divn. "G".
10. R.S.M.
11. War Diary.
12. War Diary.
13. File.

Ref.
Map
MONTBREHAIN
1/20,000

Appendix No 6

AMENDMENT No. 1. to OPERATION ORDER No. 29.

SECRET.

Copy No. 13

1. The attack upon VILLERS Farm will now be carried out by 1st Bn. K.O.Y.L.I. At the same time as this attack as ~~this attack~~ is launched a Bn. of the 38th Divn. will form up on their right and will attack VILLERS OUTREAUX from the South. The whole operation will be under the orders of G.O.C. 151 Inf. Bde. and not under G.O.C. 149th Inf. Bde.

2. H.Q. 151 Inf. Bde. is established at VAUXHALL QUARRY at which point O's. C. "B" & "D" Coys. will report at once.

3. They will synchronise watches after 18.00 at 151 Inf. Bde. H.Q.

Issued at 18.35 hours.
7th October, 1918.

Major.
Adjt. 50th Bn. M.G.Corps.

Reference
Map France
Sheet.
57 b

50th Bn. M.G.C. ORDER No. 30.

SECRET.

Copy No. 13.

Attention

1. The South African Brigade of the 66th Division will relieve the left Bn. of the 50th Division and all machine guns in Q.2., Q.7., Q.8., and Q.9., on the evening of the 14th October.

2. Details of relief will be arranged between O.C. "D" Coy., and O.C., "C" Coy. 25th Machine Gun Bn.
   If more convenient a direct relief by 100th Machine Gun Bn., who will subsequently be taking over from the 25th Machine Gun Bn., can be arranged.
   On completion of relief O.C. "D" Coy., will retain his existing H.Qrs. in NEUBOIS, where all sections relieved will be billeted.

3. The 50th Division is taking over from the 27th American Division in Q.34.a.5.5.
   Further orders will be issued in the event of a machine gun relief in that area.

4. On completion of relief O.C. "A" Coy., will assume command of all the guns in the line.

Issued at 1326 hrs.
14th October, 1918.

A. Devine
Major.
Adjt. 50th Bn. M.G.Corps.

Copies to :-

1. C.O.
2. 2nd Command.
3. Signal Officer.
4. Qr. Mr.
5. "A" Coy.
6. "B" Coy.
7. "C" Coy.
8. "D" Coy.
9. 150th Inf. Bde.
10. 25th M.G. Bn.
11. 100th M.G. Bn.
12. War Diary.
13. " "
14. File.

SECRET.
Copy No. 10.

PRELIMINARY INSTRUCTIONS for OPERATIONS to take place on Z Day.

INFORMATION. 1. At a date and an hour to be notified later the Fourth Army will continue its advance in which the 50th Divn. will co-operate. The 27th American Divn. will attack on the right, and the 66th Divn. will take LE CATEAU and the high ground in K.36. on the left.

BOUNDARIES. 2. The Divnl. boundary on the right will be a straight line from Q.27.b.9.3. to R.9.b.0.2., and on the left from road junction at Q.9.c.8.4., to junction of road and railway in K.35.c., thence to road junction at K.35.d.7.0., thence along road to K.36.d.4.8.

OBJECTIVES. 3. The following are the objectives assigned to the Divn.

(1) High ground from about R.13.d.3.5., to K.36.d.4.8.

(2) A line from about R.9.b.0.2., along N.E. of Orchards, through R.1.b. and a., to about L.31.c.0.0.

(3) An intermediate objective on the road running through Q.23, Q.17, Q.10, where a pause of two hours will take place, in order to enable the troops on the right to come up into line.

TROOPS TAKING PART. 4. 151st Inf. Bde. will attack on the right; its left on the intermediate objective being approximately Q.11.c.3.0.

149th Inf. Bde. will attack on the left.

The attack will be supported by Artillery, Machine Guns and tanks.

ORDERS to TROOPS. 5. Two Bn.s M.G.Corps will be employed to cover the advance, and will take up the following approximate positions :-

(a) 24 guns 199th M.G.Bn., under Major WHEATLEY, will establish battery positions approximately at Q.27.d.0.0., Q.27.central, Q.21.c.8.0, and will open fire at Zero on the ditch running from Q.29.a.60.15 - Q.25.c.4.0 - Q.22.d.45.80, and will search ravine running N.E. to Q.23.a.9.0. At Zero plus Y, guns firing on ditch from Q.29.a.60.15 - Q.23.c.4.0, will lift on to ditch running from Q.29.b.6.9 to Q.25.c.4.0. At the same hour all other guns will lift 200 yards.
At Zero plus Y plus X all guns will fire on the general line Q.29.b.6.9 - Q.17.c.44.50.
At Zero plus Y plus X plus W, all guns will cease firing.
Group Commanders command post about Q.28.d.40.75.

(b) 16 guns "B" Coy. and 12 guns "C" Coy., 50th M.G.Bn. will establish battery positions about Q.21.central and Q.15.c.6.6., and will open fire at Zero on the following targets :-
Tracks and sidings in Q.10.central, Brickworks in Q.10.d., Factories in Q.4.c., and Q.10.a.
At Zero plus Y all fire will be lifted to the general line Q.10.d.6.8 - Q.4.d.0.0. - Q.4.c.6.8. At Zero plus Y plus X all guns will cease fire, and will be prepared to fire on S.O.S. lines N.E. of road from Q.17.d.6.2. - Q.10.b.8.0.
Group Commanders H.Q. Q.29.b.5.2. or Q.23.b.9.5. to be decided by reconnaissance.

(c) 32 guns 199th M.G.Bn., under Major MIDDLETEY and Major MILLS, will be established in By. positions in Q.8., and Q.3., to deal with the following targets :-
Railway siding in Q.10. Brickworks at about Q.10.d.8.8., Road junction at Q.4.b.4.9., South bank of railway from Q.6.a.0.1 - Q.5.c.2.9., area in K.35.c., S. of road running E.S.E. to K.36.c.8.5.

page 2.

At Zero plus Y, all guns will lift off the three first targets and will be concentrated on remaining targets. At Zero plus Y plus X, all guns will cease fire and will be prepared to cover infantry holding line of road from Q.10.b.8.0 - Q.4.d.4.1, if called upon to do so.
Group Commanders C.P. about Q.2.d.0.0.

(d) O.C. "D" Coy., 50th M.G.Bn., will concentrate all guns and fighting limbers in valley in Q.27.s., and will establish a report centre about Q.28.d.40.75, jointly with (a) Group Commander. At Zero plus 40 he will move forward to Q.28.b. and d., and at Zero plus 3 hrs. 20 mins. will have battery positions established so as to open fire on the general line R.19.a.7.0 - Q.18.central - Q.18.b.8.0. At Zero plus 3 hrs. 35 mins., all guns will lift 300 yards and at Zero plus 3 hrs. 40 mins., all guns will cease fire. O.C. "D" Coy. will be prepared at any moment after Zero plus 3 hrs. 20 mins., to assist in the establishment of a defensive flank along the approximate line R.13.d.0.0. - Q.24.central. He will co-operate with 151 Inf. Bde. H.Q., Q.19.central.

(e) O.C. "A" Coy. will concentrate all his guns (including one section "C" Coy. attached) in valley in Q.21.s. and c., and will establish his H.Q. at Q.20.b.9.5., or Q.20.b.5.2., to be decided by reconnaissance. At Zero plus 60 he will move forward to railway sidings about Q.10.b.2.6., detaching one section to cover re-entrant in Q.17.central. From the railway siding he will bring all possible fire to bear on R.35.c., and d., until Zero plus 3 hrs. 45 mins., at which hour he will switch on to the general line R.1.c.3.0. - L.31.c.0.0. At Zero plus 3 hrs. 55 mins., he will lift 300 yards, and at Zero plus 4 hrs. 5 mins. will cease fire. He will co-operate with 149 Inf. Bde. H.Q., Q.19.central.

(f). (b) Group Commander will concentrate all guns, and at Zero plus 3 hrs., will move forward to the general line LA ROEX Fme., R.7.a.0.0. - Q.6.central, which he will consolidate in depth. Two sections will be held in readiness to support the advance of the reserve (150) Inf. Bde. to the final objective. He will establish a report centre at le QUENNLET CHANGE for the purpose of receiving orders.

RECONNAISSANCES. 6. Group Commanders will carry out reconnaissances as soon as possible, and will report battery positions selected.

COMMUNICATIONS. 7. O.C. 50th Bn. M.G.C. Signal Section, jointly with O.C. 100th Bn. M.G.C. Signal Section, will arrange to lay lines to the following points :-

(a) Joint Bde. H.Q., Q.19.d.1.9.
(b) Q.20.b.4.5. or Q.20.b.5.2. (to be decided after reconnaissance)
(c) Q.2.d.0.0.
(d) Q.28.d.40.75.

and will establish the following runners posts :-
(a) le QUENNLET CHANGE.
(b) Q.27.s.0.0.
(c) Q.19.c.0.4.
(d) Q.20.b.8.5. (or Q.20.b.5.2.) as may be decided after reconnaissance.)
(e) Q.19.d.1.9.

He will also endeavour to establish visual stations in Q.26, Q.28, and R.23.

page 3.

GAS PRECAUTIONS. 8. At every point of concentration a liberal supply of Chloride of Lime will be installed. Officers and men will be warned that if their positions is shelled a mixture of H.E. and Gas is almost certain.

TOOLS. 9. Each gun team detailed to move forward will carry three shovels.

H.Q. 10. Bn. H.Q. will remain at HONNECHY where all messages will be sent.

A Devey
Major & Adjt.
50th Bn. M.G. Corps.

15th September, 1918.

Copies to :-

1. C.O.
2. 2nd in Command.
3. Signal Officer.
4. Qr. Mr.
5. "A" Coy.
6. "B" Coy.
7. "C" Coy.
8. "D" Coy.
9. XIII Corps M.G.Officer.
10. War Diary.
11. War Diary.
12. File.
13. 50th Division "G".
14. 100th M.G.Bn.
15. 149 ⎫
16. 150 ⎬ Inf. Bdes
17. 151 ⎭
18. 25th Bn. MGC
19. 27th American Divn.

Reference
Map FRANCE
Sheets 57b N.E. & 57b S.E.
S 1/20,000.

Appendix No 9

50th Bn. M.G.C. ORDER No. 31.

SECRET.

Copy No. 1

INFORMATION. 1.   See Preliminary Instructions.
The attack will take place on the 17th October.
Zero hour will be notified later to those concerned.

BOUNDARIES. 2.   See instructions already issued.
Objectives 4 The advance from the intermediate objective to the first
objective will now take place at Zero plus 2 hrs. 12 mins.

TROOPS TAKING
PART. 4.   The 151st Inf. Bde. will now be responsible for the
whole of the intermediate objective. The first objective
will be taken by 149th Inf. Bde; the second objective
being taken by 150th Inf. Bde.

ORDERS to
TROOPS. 5.   See instructions already issued.
(a) One Coy. 18th M.G. Bn., will now take the place of 24
guns of 100th M.G.Bn.

(b) Group Commanders Command Post Q.21.c.2.8.

(c) 60 guns 100th M.G.Bn., will now be established in battery
positions in Q.8. and Q.3., less two guns which will be
mounted at dusk at Q.9.a.5.5., to cover bridge at Q.9.b.2.0.
Additional posts will be selected in order to bring fire to
bear on road running from K.35.d.5.0. towards K.36.d.8.9.,
and on slopes in K.35.d.

(d) O.C."D" Coy. will move forward to his position immediately in rear of the last Bn. 151st Inf. Bde. He will detail
one section to command the re-entrant in Q.17.central.

(e) In view of the alteration in the time at which Infantry
advance from the intermediate objective, O.C."A" Coy. will
switch on to the general line R.1.c.3.5 - L.31.c.0.0. at
2 hrs. 37 mins. He will not detach a section to cover the
re-entrant in Q.17.central, but will be responsible for
searching a trench running from Q.11.a.0.0. - Q.5.c.6.0 to
Q.5.central., and also the wood in Q.5.c. and d. At Zero
plus 2 hrs. 47 mins. he will lift 300 yards. At Zero plus
2 hrs. 55 mins. he will cease fire. "A" Coy. H.Q. will be
at Q.20.d.3.9., and a report centre will be established at
the railway siding at about Q.10.b.2.6. The Coy. will cross
the stream in Q.15.b. by a bridge N. of railway and by
fallen trees.
(f). (b) Group Commander will establish personal liaison
with G.O.C. 150th Inf. Bde. at LE QUENNELET GRANGE. He
will detail two sections to support the advance of the
150th Inf. Bde. to the second objective. One section
moving immediately in rear of infantry will, as soon as
possible, take up positions in readiness to open fire on
road junctions at R.3.a.3.4. and R.2.d.4.6. The second
section will, as soon as possible, take up position from
which fire can be brought to bear on the valley in Q.31.d.
and b. The Group will cross the stream as is most convenient, either in Q.28.c., Q.21.b., or Q.15.b., and will move
forward at Zero plus 2 hrs. 30 mins.   150th Inf. Bde. will
not move forward to the second objective until Zero plus
6 hrs.

RECONNAISSANCES. 6.   See instructions already issued.
Battery positions and targets will be reported by 11.00
hrs. 16.10.18.

page 2.

COMMUNICATIONS. 7. See instructions already issued.
Lines will be laid to :-
(a) Q.19.d.1.9.
(b) Q.20.d.3.9.
(c) Q.2.d.0.0.
(D) Q.21.c.2.8.
(e) Advanced Divnl. H.Q. HONNECHY Station.
(f) Forward Report Centre Q.19.d.75.85.
Visual stations will be established at :-
P.23.d.6.6. (Call H.Y.)
Q.26.a.5.9. (Call F.R.)
Q.23.a.8.7. (Call Q.G.)
The first two stations will be established at Zero, and the third as soon as the situation permits :-
Runners posts will now be established at :-
Q.19.d.1.8.
Q.22.a.0.3.
Q.22.d.9.9.

GAS PRECAUTIONS. 8. See instructions already issued. O.C. 100th M.G. Bn. and O.C. 18th M.G.Bn. will arrange to draw Chloride of Lime required at Bn. H.Q., HONNECHY.

TOOLS. 9. See instructions already issued.

H.Q. 10. See instructions already issued.

SYNCHRONISATION
of WATCHES. 1. All Group Commanders will send an officer to report at Bn. H.Q. at 21.00 hrs. 16.10.18 in order to synchronise watches.

RATES of FIRE. 12. Rates of fire on various targets will be notified later.

Issued at 07.00 hrs.
16th October, 1918.

Major & Adjt.
50th Bn. M.G.Corps.

Copies to :-

1. C.O.
2. 2nd in Command.
3. Signal Officer.
4. "A" Coy.
5. "B" Coy.
6. "C" Coy.
7. "D" Coy.
8. Qr. Mr.
9. C.M.G.O. XIII Corps.
10. 50th Divn. "G".
11. 149th Inf. Bde.
12. 150th " "
13. 151st Inf. Bde.
14. 100th M.G. Bn.
15. 66th M.G. Bn.
16. 18th M.G.Bn.
17. War Diary.
18. War Diary.
19. File.

Ref: Map
Sheets 57b N.E.
57b S.E.
1/20,000.

ADDENDUM No. 1.
to
50th Bn. M.G.C. ORDER No. 31.

SECRET.

Copy No 18

Appendix No 9

ORDERS to TROOPS.
  (para 5.)   Reference Preliminary Instructions. Lifts will take place as follows :-

(a) At Zero plus 30 mins., all guns will lift to their second task, and at Zero plus 40 mins., all guns will lift to their third task: At Zero plus 55 mins., all guns will cease fire.

(b) At Zero plus 66 mins., all guns will lift to their second task and at Zero plus 75 mins., all guns will cease fire, and will be prepared to fire on S.O.S. line.

(c) At Zero plus 15 mins., battery detailed to search ravine in Q.22.d. will cease fire, and will be used as a battery of opportunity, and at Zero plus 50 mins., guns shooting on rifle pits in Q.16.b. will cease fire. At Zero plus 60 mins., guns firing on rifle pits in Q.10.d., will also cease fire and will be ready to cover infantry holding line of road from Q.10.b.8.0 - Q.4.d.4.1, if called upon to do so. At Zero plus 65 mins., all guns will lift off their first three targets laid down in preliminary instructions and will concentrate on remaining targets. At Zero plus 135 mins., all fire will cease except on observed targets.

(d) As amended verbally. O.C. "D" Coy. will establish battery positions in Q.28.b., and d., by Zero plus 80 mins., and will be prepared to cover 150th Inf. Bde. At Zero plus 135 mins. batteries will open fire on the general line B.19.a.2.8. - Q.12.d.0.0. At Zero plus 140 mins., all guns will lift 300 yards and at Zero plus 149 minutes all guns will cease fire and will be consolidated in depth in rear of the intermediate objective.
    They will be prepared to establish a defensive flank from Q.24.central to R.13.d.0.0.

Reference
Map FRANCE
Sheet
57b.

50th Bn. M.G.C. ORDER No. 23.

SECRET.

Copy No. 11

Appendix No 11

RELIEF.

1. The 25th Bn. M.G.C. will relieve the 50th Bn. M.G.C., and two Coys, 100th Bn. M.G.C., attached, in the line this evening.
 O.C. "A" Coy., 50th M.G.Bn., will withdraw without relief.
 O.C. "B" & "C" Coys, 100th M.G.Bn., will be relieved by "B" Coy. 25th M.G.Bn. Relief to be completed by 22.00 hrs., at which hour O.C. 25th M.G.Bn., will take command of machine guns in the line. Completion of relief to be notified by code message "CATEAU - hours."

DISPOSITIONS on RELIEF.

2. O.C. "A" Coy., 50th M.G.Bn., will re-occupy billets vacated in HONNECHY tonight, and will proceed tomorrow morning to MARETZ. "B" & "C" Coys., 100th M.G.Bn., will be accomodated in MAUROIS. O.C. 100th M.G.Bn., will arrange with Area Commandant, MAUROIS as to accomodation of these Coys.
 Bn. H.Q., "B", "C" & "D" Coys., 50th M.G.Bn., will proceed to MARETZ this evening under orders to be issued later.

C H Hunyer
for
Major & Adjt.
50th Bn. M.G.Corps.

Issued at 14.45 hrs.
19th October, 1918.

Copies to :-

1. C.O.
2. 2nd in Command.
3. Signal Officer.
4. Qr. Mr.
5. "A" Coy.
6. "B" Coy.
7. "C" Coy.
8. "D" Coy.
9. 100th M.G.Bn.
10. 25th M.G.Bn.
11. War Diary.
12. War Diary.
13. File.

Ref. Map.
Sheet 57b N.E.
57b S.E.
1/20,000.

50th Bn. M.G.C. ORDER No. 2.

SECRET.

Copy No. 20

Appendix No 10

ATTACK. 1. The XIII Corps will continue its advance tomorrow. The first objective will be the same as todays first objective; the second objective being a line running from R.9.c.0.2. through R.8.a.6.6., along road to Q.6.b.6.0. The attack on the first objective will be carried out by all infantry Bns., formed into three Composite Bdes., of the 50th Divn. As soon as that objective has been captured it will be consolidated. After a pause of two hours the 75th Inf. Bde. (25th Divn.) will pass through and will capture and consolidate the final objective.

TASKS of MACHINE GUNS. 2. O.C. "D" Coy. will arrange to barrage at the zero hour with a 5-gun battery :- Copse on the grid line between R.13 and Q.18, lifting 300 yards at zero plus 20 mins. At zero plus 30 mins. he will cease fire and will hold two sections in readiness to advance with the 75th Inf. Bde. to the second objective. These guns will be established as soon as possible in positions from which to barrage road junction at R.3.a.3.4, and road junction at R.2.b.4.6., and also the neighbourhood of J. JACQUES MILL, L.31.d. As soon as this objective has been captured these sections will select positions for consolidation in depth. O.C. "B" Coy., at zero hour, will arrange to barrage the following targets :- Copse in Q.12.c.; practice trenches in Q.12.d.; Copse near road on grid line between Q.11.b. and Q.12.a. At Zero plus 10 mins., all guns will lift 200 yds., and at zero plus 20 mins., all guns will cease fire and two sections will move forward, as soon as possible, to assist in the consolidation of the first objective on the approximate front R.13.d.3.5. - R.7.a.central, paying particular attention to his right flank.

O.C. "A" Coy. will arrange to barrage the high ground on the approximate line Q.12.central) Q.6.central; and at zero plus 30 mins., will lift to line R.7.a.0.0. - R.1.a.0.0. At zero plus 40 mins., he will cease fire, and will move forward two sections to consolidate the first objective on the approximate front R.7.a.central - K.36.d.5.7., paying particular attention to his left flank.

ZERO HOUR. 3. Zero hour will be 05.30 hrs.

COUNTER ATTACK. 4. O.C. 100th M.G.Bn., will continue to be prepared to deal with counter attack from K.35 and Q.5.

Issued at 23.30 hrs.
17th October, 1918.

AFTER ORDER

Major & Adjt.
50th Bn. M.G.Corps.

Personal liaison will be established at Zero hour by OC "D" Coy with GOC 75th Inf Bde. at Embankment Q.22 central in order to arrange Copse rendezvous for advance of two sections.

Copies to :-
1. C.O.
2. 2nd in Command.
3. Signal Officer.
4. ~~O~~ CMGO XIII Corps
5. "A" Coy.
6. "B" Coy.
7. "D" Coy.
8. "D" Coy.
9. XIII Corps M.G.Officer.
10. 50th Divn. "G".
11. 149th Inf. Bde.
12. 150th Inf. Bde.
13. 151st Inf. Bde.
14. 25th Bn. M.G.C.
15. "D" Coy. 18th Bn. M.G.C.
16. 100th Bn. M.G.C.
17. 66th Bn. M.G.C.
18. 27th American Divn.
19. War Diary.
20. War Diary.
21. File.

page 2.

(e) At Zero plus 135 minutes, O.C. "A" Coy. will lift on to the line of the road R.1.c.0.7., K.35.d.5.0., and at Zero plus 145 minutes will lift on to the general line R.1.c.3.5 L.31.c.0.0. At Zero plus 160 minutes he will lift 300 yards, and at Zero plus 170 minutes will cease fire and will consolidate in depth in rear of the intermediate objective in support of the left of 151st Inf. Bde.

(f) For "valley in Q.31.d. and b.", read "Valley in L.31.d. and b."

Identification trace is attached for use of recipients of O.O. 31 concerned.

Issued at 1540 hrs.
16th October, 1918.

Major & Adjt.
50th Bn. M.G.Corps.

Copies to :-

1. C.O.
2. 2nd in Command.
3. Signal Officer.
4. "A" Coy.
5. "B" Coy.
6. "C" Coy.
7. "D" Coy.
8. Qr. Mr.
9. C.H.G.O., XIII Corps.
10. 50th Divn. "G".
11. 149th Inf. Bde.
12. 150th Inf. Bde.
13. 151st Inf. Bde.
14. 100th M.G.Bn.
15. 66th M.G.Bn.
16. 18th M.G.Bn.
17. M.G.Commander, 27th Amer. Divn.
18. War Diary.
19. War Diary.
20. File.

Ref. Maps.
57b N.E. & S.E.
1/20,000.

50th Bn. M.G.C. ORDER No. 34.

SECRET.

Copy No 10

Appendix No 12

INFORMATION 1. ON Z Day at an hour to be notified later the Third and Fourth Armies will continue their advance.
The role of the Fourth Army is to form a defensive flank to the major operations conducted by the Third Army.

TROOPS EMPLOYED. 2. On the front of the XIII Corps the attack will be carried out by the 6th, 25th and 18th Divns., with the 50th and 100th Bns.M.G.C. attached for barrage purposes, the 50th M.G.Bn. covering the left of the 25th Divn,

ORDERS to COMPANIES. 3. Two groups, each of 16 guns, under the command of Major F.M. PASTEUR, M.C., and Lieut. H.A. DARLING respectively will be formed for the above purpose.
Major PASTEUR's group will consist of his own Coy., with Lieut. MEREDITH and 2nd Lieut. GREAVES, M.C. ("D" Coy.) attached.
Lieut. DARLING's group will be composed of his own Coy. and 2nd Lt. H. RENNISON attached.

TASKS of GROUPS. 4. The following tasks will be carried out :-
(a) Major PASTEUR's group will select battery positions to deal with the following targets :-
(1) J.JACQUES MILL and COPSE in L.31.c.
(2) Copse in L.31.d.
(3) Copse in L.31.c.
(4) Copse in L.31.a.
(b) Lieut. DARLING'S group will shoot :-
(5) GARDE MILL and COPSE E.N.E. of it.
(6) Road junction L.31, d.19.
(7) Roads running E.N.E. from that point to POMMEREUIL.

TARGETS at ZERO HOUR. 5. At Zero hour guns will fire as follows :-
(a) Two guns J.JACQUES Mill.
Two guns W. edge of Orchard L.31.d.6.6.
Four guns on western edge of orchard in L.31.c.
Two guns L.32.c.5.5.

TARGETS at ZERO HOUR (cont.) 5.
    Two guns L.32.c.2.8.
    Two guns L.32.a.40.15.
    Two guns L.32.a.05.60.

At Zero plus X minutes all guns will lift on to orchards in L.32.a, and at Zero plus X plus W minutes all guns will cease fire.
    One section will be held in readiness to move forward should the occasion demand.

(b) 12 guns will fire on GARDE MIll and Orchard in L.25.d.
    4 guns will fire on road junction L.31.b.9.9.

At Zero plus Y minutes 8 guns will search each road running E.N.E. to POMMEREUIL as follows :-
    Two guns L.25.d.4.0, L.25.d.55.05, L.25.d.65.10, L.25.d.75.13.
    Two guns L.31.b.35.82, L.31.b.5.9, L.25.d.72.00, L.25.d.89.00.

At Zero plus Y plus 8 minutes all guns will lift 200 yards Eastwards on their respective roads and at Zero plus Y plus 16 minutes all guns will cease fire.
    One section will be held in readiness to move forward should an opportunity for action present itself.

RATE of FIRE 6. 3 minutes - 1 belt per minute, then slow until five minutes before the cessation of fire from which time as rapid fire as possible will be maintained.

POSITION of GROUPS. 7. Number one group will take up battery positions along the E. edge of the orchard in Q.11.b. and Q.5.d.
    Number two group will be on the road in Q.6.a.

HEADQUARTERS. 8. Joint group H.Q. will be established either in the road in Q.5.c., or in the railway triangle.
    Advanced Bn. H.Q. will be established either at the station Q.10½.b.3.6. or at the Sugar Factory Q.4.c.8.5.
    Exact locations will be notified later.

COMMUNICATION. 9. O.C. Signal Section will arrange to lay two lines from Advanced Bn. H.Q. to joint group H.Q. and an extension to each group position.

page 3.

RENDEZVOUS 10. Groups will proceed by march route to the railway triangle in Q.5.a. "B" Coy. will move off from MARETZ at 13.00. "C" Coy. will move at 13.15. Cookers will be taken. Dress - Fighting Order,; Jerkins will be carried.

AMMUNITION. 11. All ammunition will be taken forward in belt boxes so as to maintain a high rate of fire.
For this purpose O's.C. "A" & "D" Coys. will place all available belt boxes less a reserve of two per gun at the disposal of O's.C. "B" & "C" Coys.

WATER SUPPLY. 12. Group Commanders will ensure that apart from the water carts an adequate supply of water is taken forward in petrol tins. Water carts will be taken, and water will be supplied to surplus personnel of "B" & "C" Coys. by O.C. "A" Coy. and O.C. "D" Coy. respectively.

Major & Adjt.
50th Bn. M.G.Corps.

Issued at 23.40 hrs.
22nd October, 1918.
21st

Copies to :-
1. C.O.
2. 2nd in Command.
3. "A" Coy.
4. "B" Coy.
5. "C" Coy.
6. "D" Coy.
7. Signal Section.
8. Qr. Mr.
9. 25th Bn. M.G.C.
10. War Diary.
11. War Diary.
12. File.

Ref: Map
Sheet 57b SE
1/20,000.

50th Bn. M.G.C. ORDER No. 35.

Appendix No 12

SECRET.

Copy No. 10

1. 50th Divn. will relieve portions of the 18th and 25th Divns. in the line on the night of the 30th/31st Oct.

2. The Bn. will move to LE CATEAU tomorrow, 29th inst.

3. Order of March. Bn. H.Q; "C" Coy. "D" Coy. "A" Coy. "B" Coy.

   Starting Point. Railway Crossing at V.1.c.6.4.

   Hour of passing Starting Point. 10.45.

   Route. BUSIGNY - HONNECHY Station.

   Distances. As laid down in Fourth Army Standing Orders will be observed as far as HONNECHY Station, after which all distances will be doubled, except that 25 yards will continue to be maintained between batches of 6 vehicles.

   Dress. Full Marching Order. Helmets to be carried on haversacks. Packs to be carried on transport.

4. The N.C.O's and men whose names have been submitted as bandsmen will parade at the Bn. Orderly Room at 09.45, and will march with Bn. H.Q. Their packs and blankets will be carried by Coys.

5. A billeting party of one mounted officer per Coy. will meet Lt. C.V. FORSLIND, M.C. at Bn. Orderly Room at 08.45.

Issued at 2140 hours.
28th October, 1918.

Major & Adjt.
50th Bn. M.G. Corps.

Copies to :-

1. C.O.
2. 2nd in Command.
3. N.C.O. i/c Signals.
4. Qr.Mr.
5. "A" Coy.
6. "B" Coy.
7. "C" Coy.
8. "D" Coy.
9. Sgt. Leggett.
10. War Diary.
11. War Diary.
12. File.

CONFIDENTIAL

Army Form W.3091.

Vol 9

Cover for Documents.

Nature of Enclosures.

50TH BN. M.G.C.
WAR DIARY
VOL. 8.

Notes, or Letters written.

NOVEMBER 1ST 1918
TO
NOVEMBER 30th 1918.

WAR DIARY or INTELLIGENCE SUMMARY

Army Form C. 2118.

(Erase heading not required.)

Place	Date	Hour	Summary of Events and Information	Remarks and references to Appendices
In the field	May 1st		D Coy relieved A. Coy, taking up same positions, three sections in defensive position and one section in reserve. Increase of hostile artillery.	OUT
			5 officers arrived from M.G. Base.	
	2nd		Intensive M.G. series D issued. Major Moore DSO attended a Conference held at Div H.Q. C.O. returned from leave. O.C. Coy reconnoitred battery position. D. Coy fired "Rose Barrage" at intervals during night.	After No 1
	3rd		C.O. attended Conference at Div H.Q. in morning. O.C. Coys reconnoitred lines A, B, C. Coys moved up to the line at about 1500 hours. Bn H.Q. moved to Becasse Avenue at 21.00. D. Coy fired "Rose Barrage" during night. 2 O.R. wounded.	COS
	4th		Enemy Coys attacks on Cinjunction with the Cato on right and left. Zero hour 06:15. All objectives gained up to time. Coys carried out barrage fire at ZERO. Received 50 O.R. in order No 262, 151 & Inf. 13 Div. Consolidated Green line. 2/Lt Pearson & 26 E.A. [illegible] wounded. 10 O.R. [illegible] 1/8th Order No 37 issued 4/4/18	After No 2 OUT OUT
	5th		Attack resumed at 06:30 hrs, 2 sections of D Coy relieved 2 sections of C Coy.	OUT

CWH

2449 Wt. W14957/M90 750,000 1/16 J.B.C. & A. Forms/C.2118/12.

Place	Date	Hour	Summary of Events and Information	Remarks and references to Appendices
	10th		of B Coy working with 149th Inf Bn. A Coy moved forward with 150 Inf Bn & D Coy with 151 Inf Bn. Bn H.Q. moved at 1700 hrs and proceeded to HACHETTE FARM. Casualties five OR wounded	
	6th		Near Bn. H.Q. & seven Coy. H.Qs moved to HACHETTE FARM. C. Coy withdrawn from 151 Inf Bn and came out to HACHETTE FARM. D Coy then in reserve sent two sections forward to support 149 Inf Bn. 151 Inf Bn went through 150 Inf Bn. B Coy in reserve at HACHETTE FARM. Bn Order No 38 issued. Received 50th Div order no 265. Casualties Nil.	Appendix No 3
	7th		C.O. left Bn H.Q. at 06.30 to reconnoitre line. Recd Bn Order No 38 Adar. Bn left HACHETTE FARM at 0930 and proceeded to TROU DE DIABLE, arriving about noon. Two minutes halts were sent out every Lt. R. Roxburgh & Lt. R.N. Seamanoke to get in touch with Div on right.	

WAR DIARY or INTELLIGENCE SUMMARY

Army Form C. 2118.

Place	Date	Hour	Summary of Events and Information	Remarks and references to Appendices
	8th		and to find out situation on our front. Enemy continued to harass the LA AVESNES - MAUBEUGE Road. Casualties 4 O.R. wounded. A Coy relieved by C. Coy. Two sections D. Coy attached to C. Coy. At 0730 the 151st Inf. Bde advanced to take previous days final objective, the main AVESNES MAUBEUGE Road, gaining objective and took up positions 300 yds east of the road. Casualties 2 Lt L. FRY wounded + 6 OR wounded.	007
	9th		A. Hostile Company under the Command of Major P.M. PASTEUR M.C. left at 10/00 and proceeded to join mobile brigade at LA SAVATE (N.E. AVESNES). C. Coy remained at SARS POTERIES and were billeted there the night. 2 Lt R. Fry died of wounds.	007
	10th		On the arrival of the "Mobile Company" at SARS POTERIES the operation was cancelled, owing to the early withdrawal of the Enemy. The Company was also billeted at SARS POTERIES for the night. Casualties Nil	

WAR DIARY
or
INTELLIGENCE SUMMARY

(Erase heading not required.)

Army Form C. 2118.

Place	Date	Hour	Summary of Events and Information	Remarks and references to Appendices
	10th		Bn. Order No 39 issued. B & C Coys moved to ST AUBIN and billets there overnight.	Appendix No 4
	11th		Ref. Bn. Order No 39 Bn. HQ A & D Coys left Trou de Diable at 10.30 hours and proceeded to ST AUBIN. Canadian of battalion at 11.00 hours.	C117
	12th		Bn. at ST AUBIN. Cleaning of billets and equipment etc undertaken.	C112
	13th		Bn. all day each Coy allotted an area to arrange work. rotated full kit. 56 recruits arrived for the Bn. Locates juir fourth during week.	C119 C117
	14th		Coys on Salvage work. a draft of 42 O.R. arrived from M.G. Corps on Salvage work. 12 recruits arrived to the Bn.	C117
	15th		A meeting of the Sports Committee took place. Corps on Salvage work. No 72632 Sgt W. Dunn awarded the M.M.	C117
	16th		Bn. Church Parade at 14.00	C117
	17th		Batt for the Bn 2/Lt M.J. O'Connor appointed M.G.	C117

WAR DIARY
or
INTELLIGENCE SUMMARY

Army Form C. 2118.

Place	Date	Hour	Summary of Events and Information	Remarks and references to Appendices
	18th		A, B & C Coys attached to 50th Div Artillery for Salvage work. 1st day of Bn Sports meeting. Weather fine	A/7
	19th		B, C, D, Coys reported to Div Artillery for Salvage work. Continuation of Bn Sports. Weather fine.	A/7
	20		Three Coys on Salvage club work Div Artillery weather fine	A/7
	21		A. C. D. Coys on salvaging the area. Weather fine	A/7
	22		Training under Coy Arrangements. Each Coy auxillers one section left to return to C.R.A., and proceed to forward area on Salvage work. The following were awarded the holiday tussel. No 458769 Pte W. Jensen R.E. at M.G.C. No 458734 Sgt. W. McGahan R.E. at M.G.C. 31849 C/O O/Sgt. E. Wheelhouse No 144920 L/C W.M. Evans. No 2331 C/O C. McGurk No 144 677 Pte W.J. Smith No 22987 Sgt W.J. Crawford. 70942 Pte J. Lamb. Weather fine & forts.	A/7

CHH

WAR DIARY or INTELLIGENCE SUMMARY

Army Form C. 2118.

Place	Date	Hour	Summary of Events and Information	Remarks and references to Appendices
	23		One Section rejoined by Coy from Salvage work. Training under Coy arrangements.	007
	24		Church parade. Lt A H Morrison & 2/Lt C C Kirk arrived from M G Base. Weather fine	007
	25		Lect. by rifles Lecture for salvage work in forward area. 29 OR arrived from M G Base. Weather fine	007
	26		Training under Coy arrangements. CO inspected chapel of Mess hut. Start of Conversion Class under 2/Lt. G. Stephens. Weather fine.	007
	27		Training under Coy arrangements. Bath for Bn. Conversion Class during the afternoon.	007
	28		Training & Conversion Class in morning. 3 ORs arrived from M.G. Base. Walk rain all day. Received Divisional Memo AC/791/9 of inst H.M. the King.	007 / 083
	29		Training & Conversion Class. 13 OR proceed to UK to take up duties. Rain all day. Bn Orders were read a portion of H.M. the King Message	after Nos 5 / 007
	30		Bn Parade and Capt Ad Major A L Y. Daring assumed Command of C Coy	007

50th Bn. MACHINE GUN CORPS. SECRET.

Copy No. 14

CORRIGENDUM No. 1.
to
INSTRUCTION No.1, SERIES D.

Para 5, b, (iii). last line. For "Sunken road in G.2.d. facing
S.E." read

"Road running through G.1.d.G.3. and G.1.d.8.9. facing SOUTH".

Issued at 0915 hrs.
3rd November, 1918.

Major.
Adjt. 50th Bn. M.G.Corps.

Copies to :-

1. C.O.
2. 2nd in Command.
3. Signals.
4. Qr.Mr.
5. "A" Coy.
6. "B" Coy.
7. "C" Coy.
8. "D" Coy.
9. 50th Divn. "G".
10. 149th Inf. Bde.
11. 150th Inf. Bde.
12. 151st Inf. Bde.
13. War Diary.
14. War Diary.
15. File.

Ref: Map.
1/20,000
Sheet 57a N.W.
and 57b N.E.

Appendix No 1

50th Bn. MACHINE GUN CORPS.

SECRET.
Copy No. 14

INSTRUCTIONS No. 1.   SERIES D.

1. OBJECT of OPERATIONS.   On a date and hour to be notified leter an operation on a large scale will be carried out with the object of breaking down the enemy's defences.

2. OBJECTIVES, BOUNDARIES and FORMING UP LINE are shown on the attached map.

3. ACTION of the INFANTRY.   The first stage of the attack will be carried out by the 149th Inf. Bde. on the right and 150th Inf. Bde. on the left.   On the completion of the first phase of the attack the red dotted line will constitute the line of resistance and the red line will constitute the outpost line.   There will be a pause after the red dotted line has been captured between Z plus 170 and Z plus 230.

The area marked on the map "to be mopped up by the 150th Inf. Bde." will be dealt with by two Coys. of 150th Inf. Bde. who will move behind a flanking barrage from S.E. to N.W. commencing two hours after Zero.   (A similar movement will be carried out by the right of the 18th Divn. simultaneously.)

The area between the red line and the yellow line will be dealt with by the 149th Inf. Bde., in conjunction with tanks during a pause which will be made when the Red Dotted line has been captured.

On completion of the first stage of the attack the 151st inf. Bde. will cross the forming up line at approximately Z. plus 3 hours and will pass through 149th and 150th Inf. Bdes. and carry out the second phase of the attack to the Green line.

4. ACTION of ARTILLERY.   The attack of 149th Inf. Bde. will be carried out under a creeping barrage moving at the rate of 100 yds. in 6 minutes.

The attack of 150th Inf. Bde. will be carried out under a creeping barrage moving at the rate of 100 yds. in 6 minutes, until the barrage reaches the edge of the BOIS de MORMAL when the barrage will lift and search the clearings in the BOIS de MORMAL and other selected targets.

The mopping up of the northern area by two Coys. of 150th Inf. Bde. will be carried out under a flanking barrage moving from S.E. to N.W.

5. ACTION of MACHINE GUNS.

(a) Guns will be distributed as follows at Zero :-

(i) 149th Inf. Bde. .... 8 guns "B" Coy.
(ii) 150th Inf. Bde. ....16 guns "A" Coy.
(iii) 151st Inf. Bde. .... 8 guns "C" Coy.
(iv) Divnl. Reserve. and primary barrage..... "D" Coy.
(v) Barrage on L'HIRONDELLE, in support of 150th Inf.Bde.
    8 guns "C" Coy. (which will rejoin "C" Coy. with 151st Inf. Bde. on completion of their task.)
(vi) Special task of supporting 25th Div. in crossing Canal.
    8 guns of "B" Coy. (which will subsequently rejoin "B" Coy. with 149th Inf.Bde. on completion of their special task.)

(b) Tasks.
(i) The guns allotted to each Bde. will act in accordance with orders issued by the Bde. to the O.C. the Coy.
(ii) 8 guns of "C" Coy. detached to support 150th Inf.Bde. will take up positions in L.12.a., and fire a standing barrage on the outskirts of the BOIS de MORMAL from G.4.c.0.8 to A.27.c.5.7.
    Duration of barrage :- Z to Z plus 36.
    Rate of fire :- 2 mins. slow.
                 2 mins. rapid.
                  32 mins. slow.
On completion of this task these guns will concentrate in FONTAINE AUX BOIS and rejoin "C" Coy.
(iii) 12 guns of "D" Coy. will take up positions in L.5.a. and c., and fire a standing barrage on the area enclosed between the roads running from A.27.a.5.2. and A.27.a.6.3., to A.20.d.4.0. and A.21.c.0.2. respectively.
    Duration of barrage :- Z to Z plus 120.
    Rates of fire :- 3 mins. slow.
                  2 mins. rapid.
                  115 mins. slow.
On completion of this task "D" Coy. will concentrate in the Sunken road in G.2.d. facing S.E.
(iv) 4 guns of "D" Coy. will take up positions in L.6.a. and c., and will bring concentrated fire to bear on the quarry at A.27.d.2.7.
    Duration of barrage:- Z to Z plus 40 mins.
    Rate of fire :- 30 mins. slow.
                 7 mins. medium.
                 3 mins. rapid.
On completion of this task these 4 guns will switch on to the targets mentioned in task iii and conform to action of remaining 12 guns of "D" Coy.

page 3.

(v) 8 guns of "B" Coy. detailed for the special task of supporting the 25th Divn., in crossing the canal will move with 149th Inf. Bde. H.Q., and, on the capture of the Red Dotted line, will perform the following task.

4 guns will move to G.17.a., or G.17.b., and will act as a battery of opportunity ~~of opportunity~~ to deal by direct fire with opposition on the south eastern side of the canal.

4 guns will take up a battery position on the high ground in G.10.d., and will search the enclosed country in G.24.b. and d.

        Duration of Barrage :- Will be notified later.
        Rates of Fire :-   do.

(These four guns will be sited primarily with a view to the consolidation in depth of the Red Dotted Line.)

These eight guns will remain under the command of O.C. "B" Coy. throughout the operation and will concentrate under his orders on the completion of their special task.

6. COMMUNICATIONS. Div. H.Q. will be at LA FAYT FARM until the capture of the Red Line when it will move to L.6.c.5.3.
On capture of Green Line Div. H.Q. will move to ROSIMBOIS.

Bn. H.Q. will be established at L.11.a.0.0. at 18.00 hrs. on Z - 1 day, and on the capture of the Green Line will move to ROSIMBOIS.

H.Q. of "D" and "C" Coys. (8 barrage guns) will be notified later.

Communication by wire will be maintained ~~established~~
(1) Between Bn.H.Q. and "D" & "C" Coy. H.Q.
(2) Between "C" & "D" Coy. H.Q.
(3) Between Bn.H.Q. and Div.H.Q.

Communication by runner and cyclist will be maintained between Bn. H.Q. and Div. H.Q. and Bn. H.Q. and all Coys.

7. S.A.A. Dump for use on and after Zero will be at L.17.a.2.1.
Demands will be made by wire either through Inf. Bdes. or M.G.Bn. H.Q., to 50th Div. "Q"., and Coys. will be ready to send transport to draw from the dump as necessary.
In emergency issue will be made on a written demand from Inf. Bde. H.Q. or M.G. Bn. H.Q.

Issued at   hrs.   Major.
2nd November, 1918.   Adjt. 50th Bn. M.G.Corps.

/ P.T.O.

Ref: Map
Sheet 57a N.W.　　50th Bn. M.G.C. ORDER No. 37.　　　　　　SECRET.
1/20,000
　　　　　　　　　　　　　　　　　　　　　　　　　　　　　　　　Copy No. 18

INFORMATION. 1.　　The 50th and 18th Divns. have reached the
　　Green Line and will continue the advance tomorrow at 06.30 hrs,
　　without a barrage.

ORDERS to TROOPS. 2.　　"C" Coy. will continue to support the
　　advance of 151st Inf. Bde., whose attack in the first instance
　　will be confined to the area between the Divnl. boundary
　　B.18.c.2.6. - CARREFOUR de L'ERMITAGE and the SAMBRE River.
　　Special attention will be paid to the right flank.
　　　　"D" Coy. will move forward at the same hour and will
　　establish positions to cover the river crossing at HACHETTE,
　　B.28.d.
　　　　"A" & "B" Coys. will conform respectively to the advance
　　of 150th and 149th Inf. Bdes., who will eventually cross
　　the river at HACHETTE, and will advance South of the marshy
　　ground in B.28, B.29, and B.30, on to the line of the railway
　　running through C.30, C.23, C.17, C.4, on which line they
　　will consolidate.　Throughout the advance O.C. "B" Coy. will
　　at all times be prepared to form a defensive flank in
　　case the progress of the 66th Divn., is delayed.who will be
　　passing through the 25th Divn., is delayed.

REPORTS. 3.　　A cyclist orderly will report at cross roads,
　　B.25.a.3.9. at 09.30 hours, and at road junction B.21.a.4.6.
　　at 12.00 hours.　Company Commanders will ensure that the
　　latest situation report and their own location and disposit-
　　ions arrive at these points at the above hours.

ADVANCED REPORT CENTRE. 4. Advanced Report Centre will be established
　　at B.25.a.3.9. by 10.00 hrs., to which point all messages
　　other than the above will be sent.

ACKNOWLEDGEMENT. 5.　　Coys. will acknowledge by bearer.

Issued at　　hrs.
4th November, 1918.　　　　　　　　　　　　　　　Major & Adjt.
　　　　　　　　　　　　　　　　　　　　　　　　50th Bn. M.G. Corps.

　　　　　　　　　　　　　　　　　　　　　　　　　　P.T.O.

Copies to :-

1. C.O.
2. 2nd in Command.
3. N.C.O. i/c. Signals.
4. Qr. Mr.
5. "A" Coy.
6. "B" Coy.
7. "C" Coy.
8. "D" Coy.
9. 50th Divn. "G".
10. 149th Inf. Bde.
11. 150th Inf. Bde.
12. 151st Inf. Bde.
13. 25th Divn.
14. 18th Divn.
15. 66th Divn.
16. C.....G.O., XIII Corps.
17. War Diary.
18. War Diary.
19. File.

Ref: Map
Sheet 57s N.W.
57a
1/20,000

50th Bn. M.G.C. ORDER No. 38.

SECRET.
COPY No. 11.

Appendix No 3

MOVE. 1. The Bn., as at present concentrated at HACHETTE Fm., will move tomorrow to Haute NUTKLES.

BILLETING PARTY. 2. A billeting representative (mounted) from "B" & "D" Coys., and from "A" & "C" Rear H.Q., will report at Bn. H.Q. at 0730 hrs. to go forward as billeting party.

STARTING POINT. 3. Level Crossing at B.27.a.9.5.

ROUTE

Bn. H.Q. pass starting point at	0956 hrs.
"D" Coy. (H.Q. and two sections)	1000 hrs.
"B" Coy.	1004 hrs.
"C" Coy. (Rear H.Q.).........	1015 hrs.
"A" Coy. (Rear H.Q.).........	1017 hrs.

ROUTE. 4. Rue des JUIFS - Rue des HAIES.

Issued at 2100 hrs.
6th November, 1918.

Lieut. & Adjt.
50th Bn. M.G. Corps.

Copies to :-

1. C.O.
2. 2nd in Command.
3. Signal section.
4. Or.Mr.
5. "A" Coy.
6. "B" Coy.
7. "C" Coy.
8. "D" Coy.
9. 50th Divn. "G".
10. War Diary.
11. War diary.
12. File.
13. R.S.M.

Ref: Map　　　　　　　　　　　　　　　　　　　　　　　　　　　　　SECRET.
Sheet 57a　　　　　　50th Bn. M.G.C. ORDER No. 39.
1/40,000.　　　　　　　　　　　　　　　　　　　　　　　　　Copy No. 9

Appendix No 4

MOVE. 1.　　　The Bn. as concentrated at BOUT de DIABLE will move
　　　　　　　to billets in D.16, 17, tomorrow.

ORDER of
MARCH. 2.　　　Bn. H.Q: "D" Coy. (two sections): "A" Coy: "C" Coy.
　　　　　　　Rear H.Q: Battle Surplus.

STARTING
POINT. 3.　　　C. 23.d.0.3.　　Head of column pass Starting point
　　　　　　　at 10.30 hrs..

ROUTE. 4.　　　MONCEAU - through C.24.b. - St. REMY-CHAUSSEE - D.14.c.
　　　　　　　and d. - St. AUBIN.

DISTANCES. 5.　Distances as laid down in A.R.O. 2037 will be maintained.

BILLETING
PARTY. 6.　　　One Officer from "A" Coy. and "D" Coy. will report to
　　　　　　　Lt. C.V. FORSLIND, M.C., at "B" Coy. H.Q., St. AUBIN at 10.00
　　　　　　　hours, for purposes of billeting.

Issued at 1900 hours.　　　　　　　　　　　　　　　　　　Capt. & Adjt.
10th November, 1918.　　　　　　　　　　　　　　　　　　50th Bn. M. G. Corps.

Copies to :-

1. C.O.
2. 2nd in Command.
3. O.C. Signals, 50th Bn. M.G.C.
4. Qr. Mr.
5. "A" Coy.
6. "B" Coy.
7. "C" Coy.
8. "D" Coy.
9. War Diary.
10. War Diary.
11. File.
12. R.S.M.
13. OC Battle Surplus

Ref: Map
Sheet 57a
1/40,000.

Appendix No 5

50th Bn. MACHINE GUN CORPS ORDER No. 40.

Copy No. 9

Reference Bn. Order No. 511.

1. For the purpose of the visit of His Majesty the King the 50th Bn. M.G.Corps will be included in the 149th Inf.Bde.Group.
2. His Majesty the King will visit the Bde. Area on Sunday, 1st prox.
3. Route through area will be the MAUBEUGE - AVESNES Road.
4. Troops of the 149th Inf. Bde. Group will assemble in the large field at N.19.b.9.5. E. of the MAUBEUGE - AVESNES Road.
5. The Bde. will form up in the field facing West.
6. The 50th Bn. M.G.Corps will be formed up on the left of the 5th Bn. R.Irish R. The formation to be adopted will be four Coys. in close column at 6 paces distance.
7. The Bde. starting point will be the entrance to the fields at N.20 a.2.5. and the 50th Bn. M.G.C. will pass the starting point at Zero plus 21 minutes. Zero hour for Sunday, 1st prox. will be notified later.
8. A practice parade will take place tomorrow, 30th inst. Zero hour will be 11.00 hrs.
9. The Bn. will parade at 0945 hrs. on the St. AUBIN - DOURLERS Road and will form up in line and will be equalised before marching off. Right of the line will be at "T" roads D.17.c.8.9. Company markers will report to the R.S.M. at this point at 0940.
10. Order of march will be "A", "B", "C" & "D". H.Q.Coy. will be split up amongst the remainder of the Bn.
11. Dress will be Jerkins with belts outside; and rifles. Waterproof sheets rolled at back of belts. Officers will NOT carry sticks.
12. Officers' chargers will not be taken into the ground but will rendezvous at a point to be selected.
13. No transport will parade.

Issued at 23.59 hrs.
29th Novr. 1918.

Capt. & Adjt.
50th Bn. M.G.Corps.

Copies to :-
1. C.O.
2. 2nd i/c.
3. "A" Coy.
4. "B" Coy.
5. "C" Coy.
6. "D" Coy.
7. H.Q. Coy.
8. War Diary.
9. War Diary.
10. File.
11. R.S.M.

Vol 10

Confidential

50th Bn M.G.C.

War Diary

Vol 9

December 1st to 31st 1918.

Place	Date	Hour	Summary of Events and Information	Remarks and references to Appendices
At Rest	8 Dec		H.M. the King wished the 50th & Division that the 50th Batt. M.G.C. and 149th Infantry Brigade were formed up in a field on the site of the main AVESNES-MAUBERGE road. 500 yards south of DOULLERS. Major J. A. MORRIS D.S.O. was in command of the Batt. Lieut. Col. C.H. HOARE D.S.O. being unable to attend. Your Majesty requested that no ceremony should take place. Dress "Walking out Dress" and leather jerkins. The Battalion was drawn up in close column of Companies with no intervals. Major J.A. MORRIS D.S.O. was presented to H.M. the King. C.S.M. G.W. WAITE DCM MM. was also presented to Your Majesty. Weather fine. 	104

WAR DIARY
or
INTELLIGENCE SUMMARY
(Erase heading not required.)

Army Form C. 2118.

Place	Date	Hour	Summary of Events and Information	Remarks and references to Appendices
	Feb.		Parades and Educational Classes in morning. Sgt F.P. COOPER and 2 guests A.E. HIGGS arrived from M.G. Base Depot also 41 other ranks. 50th Division warning order No 265 received. Weather fine but very cold.	117
	3		Received 50th Div. Movement Order No 166 ref move to DOMPIERRE on the 5th inst. No 887.14 Sergt J.S. KELLY M.M. in order to M.M. Weather very dull, light rain most of day.	117
	4		G.O.C. 50th Div inspected the Batt'n and presented medal ribbons to 16 other ranks and inspected the transport & cooking of the Battalion. 50th Batt. M.G.C. order No 41 issued. Weather. Light rain all day.	117 App. No 1

M Morris

WAR DIARY
or
INTELLIGENCE SUMMARY

(Erase heading not required.)

Army Form C. 2118.

Place	Date	Hour	Summary of Events and Information	Remarks and references to Appendices
	Dec 5		Ref. Batt. Order No. 41. The Battalion left ST AUBIN at 09.30 hours arriving at DOMPIERRE at about 11.30 hours	117
	6		Cleaning of Billets &c. Rain in afternoon.	117
	7		Educational Classes and Training. Lieut Col. C.H. HOARE D.S.O. lectured to the Battalion on the General Election. Weather, Fair.	117
	8		Church Service. Weather, Fair.	117
	9		10 Other Ranks arrived from M.G. Base. Educational Classes & Training. Weather, Rainy.	117

WAR DIARY
or
INTELLIGENCE SUMMARY

Army Form C. 2118.

Place	Date	Hour	Summary of Events and Information	Remarks and references to Appendices
	Dec 10		Lieut. E.R. NICOLL SEAFRANCKE. A+S.H. & RS. a/H M.G.C. sick Lieut. R. ROXBURGH. H.L.I a/H M.G.C. awarded M.C. Educational Classes and Training. Weather Fair	04
	11		Commanding Officer inspected Draft Educational Classes and Training Weather Rain, morning	04
	12		C.O. proceeded on leave to METZ. Major A.L.V. DERING assumed command. Educational Classes and Training in morning. Lieut. Col. A. K. GRANT DSO lectured to the Battalion, Subject " Battalions Tour of Empire and fluctuations on the Western Front. Weather Fair	04

WAR DIARY or INTELLIGENCE SUMMARY

Army Form C. 2118.

Place	Date	Hour	Summary of Events and Information	Remarks and references to Appendices
	Sept		Educational classes & training in the morning. Recreational training in the afternoon. The 59th Batt. football team played 1/2 N.F.A. result a Draw. Weather fair.	OA
	14		Training under Battalion arrangements. Educational classes. Recreational training and Running in afternoon. Lieut. D.R. MEREDITH, Royal Scots att. M.G.C. awarded M.C. Major A.W. DERING attended Conference at Divisional Canteen. Weather, fair.	OA
	15		Church parade. Battalion Order No 42 issued, ref. move to SAULTAIN. Weather, fair.	App 42.2 OA

Moore

WAR DIARY
or
INTELLIGENCE SUMMARY

Army Form C. 2118.

(Erase heading not required.)

Place	Date	Hour	Summary of Events and Information	Remarks and references to Appendices
	Dec		Instructions re Order to Entrain re-issued. Packing of limbers in preparation for Move. Received orders from Division postponing move to SAULTAIN. Weather fair	W.
	17		2/Lieut. E.A.W.WELLER. R.WAR.REGT Sect. M.G.C. (died of wounds) and 2/Lieut. L.FRY. Royal Scots Sect. M.G.C. (died of wounds) awarded M.C.	
	18		20 Recruits arrived from M.G.C. Base Depot. Training and Educational Classes in morning. Recreational training in the afternoon. Weather Stormy all day. Course for Senior N.C.O's. arranged (Duties of N.C.O.) Training and Educational Classes under Battalion arrangements. 6 Recruits proceeded to 21 M.G. as Gunners. Weather rain morning. Fair afternoon	OV7

Moore

Army Form C. 2118.

WAR DIARY
or
INTELLIGENCE SUMMARY

(Erase heading not required.)

Instructions regarding War Diaries and Intelligence Summaries are contained in F. S. Regs., Part II. and the Staff Manual respectively. Title Pages will be prepared in manuscript.

Place	Date	Hour	Summary of Events and Information	Remarks and references to Appendices
	Dec 19		Packing Limbers &c in readiness for Move to new area. Weather fair all day.	C14.
	20		Ref Batt. Order No 42. The Battalion marched from DOMPIERRE to MAROILLES. arriving there about 14.00 hours. Weather fine.	C14.
	21		Ref. Batt. Orders No 42. The Battalion marched from MAROILLES to VILLERS POL arriving about 15.00 hours. G.O.C. 50 DIV inspected the Battalion marching through LE QUESNOY. C.O. returned from PARIS leave. Weather fine all day.	C14.
	22		Ref Batt. Order No 42. The Battalion marched from VILLERS POL to SAULTAIN arriving at 14.00 hours. Owing to shortage of Billets at SAULTAIN, 2 Companies were billeted at ESTREUX. Billets at SAULTAIN. Weather fair all day.	C14.
	23		Cleaning of Billets &c in afternoon. Weather, rain in morning. Cleaning of Billets &c.	C14.
	24		2/Lt O'Rourke (Miners) left for the Battalion for UK. Training & Educational Classes in morning, Recreational Training in afternoon. Weather fair.	C14.

WAR DIARY or INTELLIGENCE SUMMARY

Army Form C. 2118.

Place	Date	Hour	Summary of Events and Information	Remarks and references to Appendices
	Dec 25		Voluntary Church Parade. Weather fine	A14
	26		2nd Lieut J.H. TARVIS arrived from R.B. Base and was posted to "D" Company. Training carried out. Weather wet	C14
	27		Lieut Col. C.H. HOARE D.S.O. proceeded on leave to U.K. Major T. MORRIS D.S.O. returned from leave and took over command. Training and Educational classes morning. Recreational training in afternoon. Weather fair all day.	C14
	28		Training & Education in morning. Recreational training in afternoon. Weather. Rain most of day.	A14
	29		"D" Company on Salvage Party. The remainder of Battalion Training and Education. Weather. Rain during morning.	C14
	30		Training and Education. Clearing up morning. "B" Company on Salvage Duty. Weather. Rain all day.	C14
	31		Training & Education. Clearing during morning. "C" Company on Salvage Duty for the day. Weather. Very fine.	C14

Ref: Map
57a
1/40,000

Appendix No 1

50th Bn. M. G. C. ORDER No. 41.

SECRET.
Copy No. 10

1. **MOVE.** The Bn. will move to DOMPIERE tomorrow, 5th December 1918.
2. **ROUTE.** Via LA BODELEZ.
3. **STARTING POINT.** Road junction D.22.b.5.7.
4. **ORDER OF MARCH.** H.Q. Coy., "B", "D", "A", "C". H.Q. Coy. will pass the starting point at 0930 hrs.
5. **DISTANCES.** As laid down in S.S.724 will be maintained.
5. **TRANSPORT.** Under Lt. C. I. Peacock will move in rear of column in the following order:- H.Q., "B", "D", "C".
6. **DISTANCES.** As laid down in S.S.724 will be maintained.

7. **DRESS.** Fighting Order.

8. **STORES.** All tables, forms, corrugated iron sheets, material for ovens, latrine fixtures, etc., will be taken. Any Stores which cannot be carried in the regimental transport will be dumped by 0800 hours at the Bn. Qr. Mr. Stores.

9. **LOADING PARTY.** The duty Coy. will provide two N.C.O's and 10 man as loading party and these will report to the Qr. Mr. at 0800 hrs. They will move to DOMPIERE under the orders of the Qr. Mr. Stores dumped at the Bn. H.Q. Stores will be transported to DOMPIERE by lorries and Coys. will arrange to re-draw their stores at the new Bn. Qr. Mr. Stores, at DOMPIERE.

10. **SCHOOL FURNITURE.** The H.Q. Coy. will arrange to move the tables etc., from the Schoolroom to the Qr. Mr. Stores by 0900 hrs. tomorrow.

Issued at 1630 hrs.
4th December, 1918.

Capt. & Adjt.
50th Bn. M.G.Corps.

Copies to:-
1. C.O.
2. 2nd in Command.
3. Qr. Mr.
4. Lt. C. I. Peacock.
5. "A" Coy.
6. "B" Coy.
7. "C" Coy.
8. "D" Coy.
9. Sig Officer
10. War Diary.
11. War Diary.
12. File.

EVERY GUN NUMBER MUST KNOW

1. The number and field of fire of their Gun.
2. Ranges to all targets, whether on their front or to their flank; and Q.E. and direction for S.O.S. fire.
3. The position of, and fields of fire of, their flanking guns.
4. The positions of all Infantry posts both to their front and flanks.
5. Position of their Section Head-quarters, and Company Head-quarters.
6. The position of the nearest Infantry Battalion Head-quarters, and of the Brigade Head quarters of the subsection covered by their fire.
7. Names of all localities on their immediate front, and of principal enemy trenches.
8. The position of their own front line, and of the enemy front line.
9. Number of rounds to be reserved, in all circumstances, for direct fire.

--------- o O o ---------

Ref: Sheet
57a and
VALENCIENNES 12.

50th Bn. MACHINE GUN CORPS ORDER No. 42.

SECRET.

Copy No. 4

1. The Battalion will move to CURGIES in accordance with attached march table.

2. Transport under Lieut. C.V. FORSLIND, MC., will move in rear of the column. Order of march will be same as Coys.

3. Signals Officer will arrange to synchronise watches with C.O. Coys. prior to each move.

4. Billeting Parties - Special instructions will be issued in regard to these.

5. Surplus stores, tables, forms, etc., which cannot be carried on the regimental transport will be sent to the yard at Bn. H.Q. mess by 0800 hrs. on the 17th December and stacked in separate Coy. dumps. These will be moved by lorries.
   A loading party of one N.C.O. and two men from each Coy. will report to the Qr.Mr. in the yard at 0730 hrs. 17th December, and will accompany the lorries. These loading parties will be rationed for the day.

6. Billeting certificates will be rendered to the Qr.Mr. by 2000 hrs. tomorrow, 16th December, 1918.

7. Dress - ~~Full Marching~~ Fighting Order.

Issued at 20.00 hrs.
15th December, 1918.

Capt. & Adjt,
50th Bn. M.G.Corps.

Copies to :-

1. C.C.
2. 2nd in Command.
3. Qr. Mr.
4. Signals Officer.
5. Lt. C.V. Forslind. MC.
6. H.Q Coy.
7. "A" Coy.
8. "B" Coy.
9. "C" Coy.
10. "D" Coy.
11. R.S.M.
12. War Diary,
13. War Diary.
14. File.

MARCH TABLE.

Date.	From.	To.	Route.	Starting Pt.	Time.	Order of March.	Remarks.
17th Dec.	DOMPIERRE.	MAROILLES.	TAISNIERES H.18.b.	"T" Roads at I.12.c.9.8.	11.30 hrs.	H.Q., "B", "C", "D", "A".	
18th Dec.	MAROILLES.	VILLERS POL.	HACHETTE. LOCQUIGNOL. LE QUESNOY.	Road Junction at H.11.4.5. H.11.c.4.5.	0755 hrs.	H.Q., "C", "D", "A", "B".	To be clear of LOCQUIGNOL by 1000 hrs.
19th Dec.	VILLERS POL.	CURGIES.	JENLAIN.	Details later.		H.Q., "D", "A", "B", "C".	Destination may be altered to SAULTAIN.

Distances. Distances as laid down in S.S. 724 will be maintained.

Halts. Hourly halts of ten minutes, ten minutes before the hour will be made.

Appendix No II

To
All Recipients of
C.O. No. 42.

Copy No. 12

Reference 50th Bn. Machine Gun Corps Order No. 42.dated 15th December, 1918. -

1. The destination (provisional) is now SAULTAIN.

2. <u>Transport</u> - Coy. Cookers will march at the head of the transport column.

3. <u>Billeting Parties.</u> One Officer, mounted, per Coy. will report at <u>Bn. H.Q. at 0830 hrs.</u> tomorrow to go forward for billeting purposes. The senior Officer will be in charge and will be responsible for billeting Bn. H.Q. as well as his own Coy.
Billeting party tomorrow will proceed to MARCILLES and report to the Area Commandant and will arrange to meet the Bn. on its arrival.
The senior Officer will report to the Adjutant before marching off.

4. <u>Lorries, Surplus Stores, etc.</u> With reference to para 5 of Operation Order No. 42, surplus stores, tables, etc., therein referred to will now be dumped as stated by 1700 hrs. today, 16th December, 1918. Bn. H.Q. will arrange to furnish a guard over these dumps during the night.
Lorries are now timed to leave at 0700 hrs tomorrow, 17th December, and will proceed direct to SAULTAIN. Loading parties will accompany the lorries and these parties will now be rationed for three days. In view of the fact that the lorries will proceed direct to SAULTAIN you will arrange to carry the stores you will require during the three days march of the Bn. in your regimental transport and send stores which will not be required by lorry. Loading parties will report to the Qr.Mr. at 0700 hrs.

5. With reference to the march table the time of passing the starting point on the 18th December will now be 0745 hrs.

Issued at 1005 hrs.
16th December, 1918.

Capt. & Adjt.
50th Bn. M.G.Corps.

CONFIDENTIAL

WAR DIARY

50TH BATT M.G. CORPS

VOL IX

JANUARY 1919.

Army Form C. 2118.

WAR DIARY
or
INTELLIGENCE SUMMARY
(Erase heading not required.)

Instructions regarding War Diaries and Intelligence Summaries are contained in F. S. Regs., Part II and the Staff Manual respectively. Title Pages will be prepared in manuscript.

Place	Date	Hour	Summary of Events and Information	Remarks and references to Appendices
SAULTAIN	Jan 1st		No parade. Recreational training in afternoon. Fine all day.	COA
	2nd		Training and education in morning. Recreational training in afternoon. Very fine.	COA
	3rd		One Company on Salvage duty, training & education in morning and recreational training in afternoon for remainder of Bn. Rain most of day.	COA
	4th		Salvage carried out by duty Company. Bn. in Training and Recreational training in afternoon. Rain in morning, fair in afternoon.	COA
	5th		Church parade. Two O.R. arrived from M.G. Base depot. Fine.	COA
	6th		Training and education in morning. Recreational training in afternoon. Fine all day. 5 O.R. proceeded to U.K. for demobilization.	COA

Maxwell Mayor

WAR DIARY or INTELLIGENCE SUMMARY

Army Form C. 2118.

Place	Date	Hour	Summary of Events and Information	Remarks and references to Appendices
SOLTAU	Sep 7th		Bn in Salvage all day. 5 O.R. proceeded to U.K. for demobilization. Fine.	C.H.
	8th		Bn on Salvage work. Very fine. Hot all day.	C.H.
	9th		Bn carried out Salvage work. Fine, very cold.	C.H.
	10th		Training & education during morning. Recreational in afternoon. Nil O.R. arrived from M.G. Base depot. Fair, very cold.	C.H.
	11th		Training & education in morning. Recreational training in afternoon. Rain all day. 5 O.R. proceeded to U.K. for demobilization. 1 O.R. proceeded.	C.H.
	12th		Church Parade. 7 O.R. arrived from M.G. Base depot. 1 O.R. proceeded to U.K. for demobilization. Fine.	C.H.
	13th		One officer and twenty four O.R. proceeded to U.K. for demobilization. D.A.D.R. inspected all arrivals of the Bn. Fair, very cold.	C.H.

J. Moore

Army Form C. 2118.

WAR DIARY
or
INTELLIGENCE SUMMARY
(Erase heading not required.)

Instructions regarding War Diaries and Intelligence Summaries are contained in F. S. Regs., Part II. and the Staff Manual respectively. Title Pages will be prepared in manuscript.

Place	Date	Hour	Summary of Events and Information	Remarks and references to Appendices
SAULTAIN	Jan 14th		One Company on Salvage work. Training and education in morning, and recreational training in afternoon. Two O.R. proceeded to U.K. for demobilisation. fair	C.M.
	15th		Training and education for Bn. in morning. Recreational training in afternoon. Snow all day.	C.M.
	16th		Training and education for Bn. in morning. Recreation in afternoon. Rain most of day.	C.M.
	17th		One O.R. proceeded to U.K. for demobilisation. Training and education in afternoon. fair	C.M.
	18th		Two officers and six O.R. proceeded to U.K. for demobilisation. Salvage, education and training in morning. Recreation in afternoon. fair	C.M.
	19th		51 O.R. proceeded to U.K. for demobilisation. Church parade. fair	C.M.

Army Form C. 2118.

WAR DIARY
or
INTELLIGENCE SUMMARY
(Erase heading not required.)

Instructions regarding War Diaries and Intelligence Summaries are contained in F. S. Regs., Part II. and the Staff Manual respectively. Title Pages will be prepared in manuscript.

Place	Date	Hour	Summary of Events and Information	Remarks and references to Appendices
SAOLTAIN	Jan 20		Duty Company on Salvage work. C.O inspected all Company billets. Education & training in morning. Recreation in afternoon. fair.	C4
	21st		Capt MOORE M.G.C. returned to the Bn. in Demobilization and proceeded to U.K. for demobilization. Recreation in afternoon. fine.	C4
	22nd		Education and training in morning. Recreation in afternoon. Showery.	C4
	23rd		Duty Company on Colonge. Training and education in morning. Snow started to fall in evening. 17 O.R. proceeded to U.K. for demobilization. Snowed most of day.	C4
	24th		M.O lectured to the Bn. in morning.	
	25th		Education and training during morning. Recreation in afternoon. Sun was hot.	C4

M Moore

Army Form C. 2118.

WAR DIARY
or
INTELLIGENCE SUMMARY
(Erase heading not required.)

Instructions regarding War Diaries and Intelligence Summaries are contained in F. S. Regs., Part II. and the Staff Manual respectively. Title Pages will be prepared in manuscript.

Place	Date	Hour	Summary of Events and Information	Remarks and references to Appendices
SAULTAIN	Sept 26		Church Parade. Sun, but hot.	ex
	27th		Duty Company on Salvage. Training and education; fine very close.	C.H.
	28th		Education and training in morning. Sun most of day.	C.H.
	29th		Education. Raining came at in morning, but hot.	C.H.
	30th		One Company on Salvage duty. Education and training for remainder of battalion. Showery.	C.H.
	31st		Education and training during morning. Showers in evening.	C.H.

M. Morris

CONFIDENTIAL

Vol 12

Volume X

WAR DIARY
of
50TH BATTALION
MACHINE GUN CORPS

FROM 1st FEBRUARY 1919
TO 28th FEBRUARY 1919

WAR DIARY
or
INTELLIGENCE SUMMARY
(Erase heading not required.)

Army Form C. 2118

Place	Date	Hour	Summary of Events and Information	Remarks and references to Appendices
SAULTAIN	Feb. 1		Training and education during morning recreational Training in afternoon	
	2		Lt Greaves MC & 31 O.R. proceeded to U.K. for demobilisation. No church parade owing to indisposition of the padre	
	3		Education and Training during morning	
	4		Training and education in the morning, recreation in the afternoon	
	5		Duty Company on Salvage work, concentrating Salvage on the main dumps. Capt. Greaves and 23 other ranks proceeded to U.K. for demobilisation	
	6		Salvage work carried out by duty company 4 O.R. proceed for demobilisation. Sgt Instructor reported for duty from Army Gym Staff	

Moore Major
COMDG. 50TH BN. M.G.C.

Army Form C. 2118.

WAR DIARY
or
INTELLIGENCE SUMMARY

(Erase heading not required.)

Place	Date	Hour	Summary of Events and Information	Remarks and references to Appendices
SAULTAIN	FEB 7		One officer and 9 O.R. proceeded for demobilization. Training and education during the morning	
	8		Education and Training during the morning. One O.R proceeded for demobilization.	
	9		One O.R proceeded for demobilization. Church Parade in the morning	
	10		Education and Training during morning, recreation afternoon	
	11		Training and education carried out in morning	
	12		C.O. inspected billets in the morning. 12 O.R. proceeded to U.K. for demobilization	
	13		Training & education in the morning	

Comdg. 50th Bn. M.G.C.

WAR DIARY
or
INTELLIGENCE SUMMARY

Army Form C. 2118.

Place	Date	Hour	Summary of Events and Information	Remarks and references to Appendices
SAULTAIN	FEB 14		Training and education during morning	
	15		One O.R. reinforcement reported to Bn from Base Depot.	
	16		Church Parade. A draft of 15 men sent from the Bn. for E. F. C. work at Hesdin (HESDIN) for Army of occupation	
	17		Draft of 4 officers & 150 men inspected by G.O.C. 10.30 hrs	
	18		C.O. inspected the draft. 10.30 hrs C and D Coys moved to BEAUDIGNIES 07.30 hrs. by march route	
	19		C.O. inspected draft during morning	
	20		Inspection and training carried out by the draft	

Comdg. 50th Bn. M.G.C.

Army Form C. 2118.

WAR DIARY
or
INTELLIGENCE SUMMARY

(Erase heading not required.)

Place	Date	Hour	Summary of Events and Information	Remarks and references to Appendices
SAULTAIN	FEB 21		Training carried out by the draft	
	22		The remainder of Bn moved by march route to BEAUDIGNIES at 08.30 hrs and the draft to SALESCHES. Heavy rain	
	23		No church parade. B and D Coys amalgamated and to be known in future as B Coy. A + C amalgamated and called A Coy. Showery weather	
	24		Pte Jones South African Bat. lectured to the draft at SALESCHES on emigration	
	25		The draft carried out training during the day	
	26		3 O.R. proceeded to U.K. for demobilisation	
	27		5 O.R. proceeded for demobilisation. Weather very wet	
	28		The Adjutant - Capt W.S. Hinde & 21 O.R. proceeded for demobilisation. Showery weather	

Comdg. 50th Bn M.G.C.

2449 Wt. W14957/M90 750,000 1/16 J.B.C. & A. Forms/C.2118/12

Confidential

Volume XII.
Vol 13

War Diary
of
50th Battalion
Machine Gun Corps

From March 1st 1919
To   "   31st "

WAR DIARY
or
INTELLIGENCE SUMMARY

Army Form C. 2118.

Place	Date	Hour	Summary of Events and Information	Remarks and references to Appendices
BEAUDIGNIES	MARCH 1		Capt. R.J.M. Scott took over duties of Adjutant - vice Capt. W.S. Hinde, proceeded for demobilisation. C.O. inspected the "Draft" at Saleches. Summer Time came into force 23.00 hrs. Three O.R. proceeded for demobilisation.	
	2		Church parade 11.00 hrs at Saleches for the "Draft"	
	3		C.O. inspected the Transport of the Battalion	
	4		Training and recreation carried out by the Draft. Weather very wet	
	5		Orders received for 14 O.R. to report to 43rd Garrison Battn. Royal Fusiliers for duty. 2 O.R. reported for duty from Base Depot.	
	6		The Draft Coy carried out during morning Training. Instructions received to strike off strength Draft of 15 O.R. sent to E.F.C. Hesdin 16th ult.	
	7		The Draft, under orders, for the 43rd Garr. Battn. R.F. proceeded at 14.00 hrs. Sergt. Brummer, Parker & 3 O.R. proceeded for demobilisation	

Army Form C. 2118.

WAR DIARY
or
INTELLIGENCE SUMMARY
(Erase heading not required.)

Instructions regarding War Diaries and Intelligence Summaries are contained in F. S. Regs., Part II. and the Staff Manual respectively. Title Pages will be prepared in manuscript.

Place	Date	Hour	Summary of Events and Information	Remarks and references to Appendices
BEAUDIGNIES	MARCH 8		Training & recreation carried out by Draft Coy. Weather fine	
	9		Church parade at Saleches for the Draft Coy. Lt C.V. Foxland proceeded on leave to U.K.	
	10		A Court of Enquiry assembled at Bn H.Q. with Major F.M. Pasteur M.C. as President, to enquire into loss of bicycle.	
	11		Inspection of billets by C.O. 1 O.R. proceeded for demobilisation Training by the Draft Coy.	
	12		Lt Col C.H. Hoare D.S.O. rejoined from leave U.K. and assumed Command of the Battn. Major F. Morris D.S.O., 2nd in Command, proceeded	
	13		for dispersal. Heavy rain during the day	
	14		Orders received cancelling Draft for 41st Bn M.G. Corps, and instructions for a Draft of 128 O.R. to proceed to 46th Bn M.G.C.	
	15		Major A.L.Y. Denny, Capt J.A. Middleton, Lt C Wood, Lt R.G. Goldie, 2/Lt H Jackson, 2/Lt A Roworth, 2nd Lt C.K Kings proceeded for demobilisation	

Army Form C. 2118.

WAR DIARY
or
INTELLIGENCE SUMMARY
(Erase heading not required.)

Place	Date	Hour	Summary of Events and Information	Remarks and references to Appendices
BEAUDIGNIES	March 16th		No Church Parade owing to medical inspection of the Draft proceeding tomorrow	
	17		Draft of 128 O.R. proceeding to join 46th Bn. M.G.C. Lt A.H. Morrison acting as conducting officer	
	18		B Company returned from Saleoches and took over billets in Beaudignies	
	19		3 O.R. proceeded for demobilisation	
	20		Billets being unfavourable - B Coy returned to Saleoches. Instructions received that no M.G.C. officer to be demobilised without authority from XIII Corps	
	21		Orders received for 15 Officers to proceed to 46th Bn M.G.C.	
	22		Lt Col C.H. Hoare D.S.O. went on leave to Paris. Weather fine but dull	

WAR DIARY or INTELLIGENCE SUMMARY

Place	Date	Hour	Summary of Events and Information	Remarks and references to Appendices
BEAUDIGNIES	MARCH 23		No church parade in morning but voluntary service in the evening at Salesches. Very fine & sunny all day	
	24		The following officers proceeded to join 46th Bn M.G.C. — Lts Morrison, Rennison, Hyde, King; 2/Lts Fife, Lloyd & Hess.	
	25		Capt Pooley & Lt Wheeler left the Bn for the 46th Bn M.G.C. Orders received for a further draft of 100 O.R. for the 46th Bn M.G.C.	
	26		Draft of 94 O.R. proceeded to 46th Bn — remaining 6 failed to pass M.O. Weather fine	
	27		C.O. inspected wheel harness of the Battn	
	28		124 Animals arrived at Bn from various units in Divn to complete Cadre "B".	
	29		Authority received for demobilisation of Lt Col C.H. Hour D.S.O. Snowed hard	
	30		Completion of Draft — i.e. 6 O.R. proceeded to 46th Bn M.G.C. 4 O.R. went on extension of service leave & struck off	
	31		Order for transfer of Lt J.S. Tanner to 46th Bn received	

Ambrosius Major in.

Confidential

VOLUME XIII

WAR DIARY

OF

50TH BATTALION

MACHINE GUN COF

FROM APRIL 1st 1919
TO APRIL 30TH 1919

Army Form C. 2118.

WAR DIARY
or
INTELLIGENCE SUMMARY

(Erase heading not required.)

Place	Date	Hour	Summary of Events and Information	Remarks and references to Appendices
BEAUDIGNIES	APRIL 1		Lt. G.S. Janner proceeded to join 46th Bn. M.G. Corps. Instructions received for Bn. to be reduced to Cadre 'A'.	Weather - fine
	2		Lt. Col. C.H. Hoare proceeded to U.K. for demobilization, having returned from PARIS leave during the morning.	Weather - fine
	3		All animals despatched to Animal Collecting Camp.	Weather - fine
	4		Received instructions for 37 O.R.s to be despatched to 18th Bn. M.G. Corps. Major F.M. Paxton M.C. took Command of Bn.	Weather - fine
	5		37 O.R.s proceeded to join 18th Bn. M.G. Corps.	Weather - fine
	6		No Church Parade - 14 O.R.s proceeded for dispersal	Weather - fine
	7		Nos. "A" & "B" Coys amalgamated forming "Cadre" Company.	Weather - fine
	8			
	9		Capt. J.W. Bradbury, C.F. proceeded for dispersal	Weather - fine
	10		Conducting party which proceeded with Animals returned.	
	11		Lt. & Q.M. Green proceeded to join 37th Bn. M.G. Corps. 2 O.R.s proceeded to U.K. for the purpose of identifying Cadre 'B' animals. 2 Sgts & 1 Cpl to be held ready for transfer to 5th Bn. M.G. Corps	

Army Form C. 2118.

WAR DIARY
or
INTELLIGENCE SUMMARY

(Erase heading not required.)

Instructions regarding War Diaries and Intelligence Summaries are contained in F.S. Regs., Part II. and the Staff Manual respectively. Title Pages will be prepared in manuscript.

Place	Date	Hour	Summary of Events and Information	Remarks and references to Appendices
BEAUDIGNIES	April 12		No Church Parade	
	13		No Church Parade. 1 Officer & 6 O.R's proceeded for disposal. Instructions received for drafts to proceed to 5, 6 & 9 Bns. M.G. Corps.	
	14		24 O.R's proceeded to join 5th & 9th Bns M.G. Corps. Weather - fine	
	15		Request received for present of entraining strength of Cadre etc.	
	16			
	17		Received instructions regarding allotment of horses from Divisional Pool. Div. received instructions R.A.V.C. Sgt is to be despatched to Cambrai. Weather - fine but very cold	
	18		Good Friday - No Parade. Weather - very fine	
	19		R.A.V.C. Sgt proceeded to Cambrai. Draft arrived from 19th Bn M.G. Corps in error. Permission asked for reposting same. Weather - fine	
	20		No Church Parade. 4 O.R's proceeded for disposal. Weather - fine in morning, but wet & windy in afternoon	
	22		Draft posted in error forwarded to 51st Bn M.G. Corps. Lt Col W. Horsfall proceeded to join No 6 Bn M.G. Corps. Weather - very fine	

[signature]

Army Form C. 2118.

WAR DIARY
or
INTELLIGENCE SUMMARY

(Erase heading not required.)

Place	Date	Hour	Summary of Events and Information	Remarks and references to Appendices
BEAUDIGNIES	APRIL 24		2 O.R's. proceeded to join 9th Bath. G. Corps. Weather - fine	
	26		Lt. v O.R. v Brown joined Bn. from 39th Bn h.g. Corps. Weather - very wet v violent	
	27		No Church Parades. 6. O.R's. proceeded for dispersal. Weather - fine but dull v very cold	
	28		No parades owing to weather. Weather - Continued snow storms	
	30		Weather - Very wet. frost in evening	

www.ingramcontent.com/pod-product-compliance
Lightning Source LLC
Chambersburg PA
CBHW081402160426
43193CB00013B/2090